Reclaiming Our Political Roots

Reclaiming Our Political Roots

Rethinking Church in Nationalist Times

Yohan Hwang

WIPF & STOCK • Eugene, Oregon

RECLAIMING OUR POLITICAL ROOTS
Rethinking Church in Nationalist Times

Copyright © 2020 Yohan Hwang. All rights reserved. Except for brief quotations in critical publications or reviews, no part of this book may be reproduced in any manner without prior written permission from the publisher. Write: Permissions, Wipf and Stock Publishers, 199 W. 8th Ave., Suite 3, Eugene, OR 97401.

Wipf & Stock
An Imprint of Wipf and Stock Publishers
199 W. 8th Ave., Suite 3
Eugene, OR 97401

www.wipfandstock.com

PAPERBACK ISBN: 978-1-7252-5217-2
HARDCOVER ISBN: 978-1-7252-5218-9
EBOOK ISBN: 978-1-7252-5219-6

Manufactured in the U.S.A.   JANUARY 23, 2020

Unless otherwise indicated, Scripture quotations contained herein are from the New Revised Standard Version, copyright © 1989 by the Division of Christian Education of the National Council of Churches of Christ in the U.S.A. Used by permission. All rights reserved.

Scripture quotations marked ESV are from the The Holy Bible, English Standard Version®, copyright© 2001 by Crossway, a publishing ministry of Good News Publishers. Used by permission. All rights reserved.

*To my children, Ian, David and Irene,
whom I pray will serve the church with whatever gifts
they may discover they have.*

Contents

Acknowledgements | ix

1. A Disquieting Suggestion | 1
2. How We Got Here: The Rise of the State | 15
3. Where We Are: The Economy and the Fracturing of Our Lives | 31
4. Where We Came From: Theological Foundations | 54
5. Where to Go from Here: Possible Solutions | 92
   Epilogue: The Politics of the Eucharist | 139

Endnotes | 149

Acknowledgements

This project would not have been possible without the support and dedication of my wife, Grace. Every married person knows that one's time is not wholly one's own. Thus one's accomplishments are always shared accomplishments. Every hour I devoted to this project meant that Grace had to take on my share of family duties. Unlike college professors who get paid to do this, I took this on as a full-time high school teacher. With two young children at home, this project engrossed not only my time but also Grace's. Yet she warmly and graciously supported me throughout the process. I am therefore deeply grateful for her faith in the project. Every word on these pages I owe to her.

I am also deeply indebted to the numerous teachers and scholars who have influenced my thoughts. Two in particular who have influenced this work are Stanley Hauerwas and William Cavanaugh. Their thoughts on political theology permeate these pages through and through. Reading Hauerwas has changed my life.

All of that influence has been an integral part of the education I have received from various institutions. And for that I am deeply grateful to my parents, who have encouraged and supported my education. I suspect they will not always agree with the contents in these pages, but I am who I am because of them.

ACKNOWLEDGEMENTS

I would also like to thank the team at Wipf and Stock: Joshua Little, Matt Wimer, Nathan Roads, George Callihan, Rachel Saunders, Savanah Landenholm, Zech Mickel, Daniel Lanning and Joe Delahanty. This project would not have come to life without their support and dedication to this work.

Finally, I would like to thank Karen Campbell and Mike Morrell, who have been invaluable in spreading the word around about the importance of this work.

1.

A Disquieting Suggestion

Imagine that the churches were to suffer the effects of a catastrophe. A series of wars are blamed on religious leaders. Widespread riots occur. Churches are razed to the ground, religious leaders executed, sacred texts burned and artifacts destroyed. Finally a political movement takes hold that abolishes the teaching of Christianity in schools and public assemblies. Generations later, there is a reaction against this destructive movement and an attempt to recover long-lost church practices takes place. Clinging to the remaining fragments that they have, the spiritually minded start to assemble once a week. Adults listen attentively to one among them who provides motivational advice. Their youth put their hands up and chant songs about running into the Father's arms. After the meeting is over, they go back to the seclusion and safety of their homes, some of which are significantly larger than others'. The following morning some go to work for the government of their nation, most for a large corporation, while others don't have any work to go to. All the while they do this not knowing how their work bears any relationship with their church. Then they come back together the following week for the same routine. Yet nobody among them realizes that what they are doing is not church, at least not in the sense that it used to be.

Some readers will recognize a striking resemblance between my opening paragraph and that of Alasdair McIntyre's *After Virtue*. McIntyre's story envisaged a catastrophe in which the study of the natural sciences was destroyed. Those that later tried to recover it were not really practicing science in the proper sense, though they thought they were. In that story, children were taught to memorize the periodic table or recite Euclid's theorem, failing to even conceive of the scientific method. Then McIntyre goes about to argue that such is the state of moral philosophy today. What passes today as ethics is framed by individualism, often leading to unresolvable conundrums, whereas in the past morality had always been shaped by the virtues acquired by the habits of a community.

But while McIntyre's story was merely an analogy between the natural sciences and the current state of moral philosophy, the story I opened with in some ways illustrates what the church has *actually* undergone in the last few hundred years, of which individualism is merely one of the ailing symptoms. We go to "church" in which we do all kinds of churchy things, and we think that our churches are genuine on the most part. But what we often call "church" today would in many ways be unrecognizable to the early Christians. If we fail to perceive that there is something rather odd and somewhat dysfunctional about the way we do church today, I suppose it must be because we and our churches have been so conformed to the patterns of this often perverse world.

Even if we failed to recognize the oddity about the way we do church, there are clear signposts right under our noses that something is truly amiss. For one, the churches in the West are in a precipitous decline. Of course, this should not be a surprise when speaking of the European church. We have heard the stories of church buildings sold to nightclubs as memberships decline. But the American church in decline? Americans have always been known as a deeply religious people. Yet data shows an unmistakable pattern of shrinking numbers across all major Christian groups. The percentage of adults in America who describe themselves as Christians was 78.4 percent in 2007 and dropped to 70.6 percent in 2014, nearly 8 percentage points down in just seven years.[1] U.S. population growth due to immigration during those years does not account for that change as the total estimated number of Christians also went down from 178 million to 172.8 million within the same years.[2] Of all factors, it is millennials, of which I am one, who are leading the pack—downward of course. Among older Christians, those born from 1928 to 1945, 85 percent identified as Christians, while merely 56 to 57 percent of millennials did so.[3]

But an aging congregation is merely a symptom of something larger ailing the church. Consider the increasing political polarization within the church. Starting from the heated 2016 election season, many Christians have unfriended each other in person (and on Facebook) over their political disagreements. Some have even left their church to join another one, or have left the institution altogether in disillusionment. I have sadly witnessed this among friends and church members. It's to the extent that Christian writers had to produce magazine pieces advising fellow Christians not to do so.[4] Isn't there something rather odd about people placing American politics first over the unity of the church? We may think this is a very recent trend brought about by the 2016 election, but this polarization has actually been broadening gradually until it reached its apex in 2016. From the 1970s to the present there has been a developing correlation between religious service attendance and political conservatism.[5] This may provide a hint as to why the younger are abandoning church faster, as they usually hold more liberal views compared to their parents, but it certainly is not the whole picture.

More importantly, there seems to be something missing in many Christians' quotidian life that eventually leads to dissatisfaction. The many facets of our lives are so fractured that we do not know how to relate our job, science, education, family, politics, and finances to the life of the church. Yet we sense that we should be able to put the pieces together somehow. As the Scriptures say, God's plan is "to gather up *all things* in him [Christ], things in heaven and things on earth"[6] (Eph 1:10). Yet we have no clue where to start. Church is for many only a thing to go to on Sundays for one or two hours. The rest of the week is spent grinding anywhere between forty to eighty hours in a government job, some corporation, or getting an education. Many just hate their jobs simply because it is so mundane, or because they feel like a mere cog in a massive money-making capitalist machine that exploits people and the environment. For those that do love their job, they do so because they find meaning, purpose, virtue and a community in their workplace, but they have a hard time finding those at church—it's only for a couple hours a week after all. No wonder why young people find the church to be decreasing in relevance.

NOT GETTING THE PROBLEM

Numerous attempts have been made to make church more appealing to younger generations, but as the data shows, much to no avail. Church membership actually started to shrink a few decades ago. To battle the trend, some pastors were on a mission to attract and retain their youth.

Congregations started to switch to more contemporary worship styles. They became seeker sensitive, meaning that they did not want to offend people on the fence. Some sanctuaries even took down their crosses, which were replaced by massive screens and theatrical lighting. The founders of these churches of course had the best of intentions (at least I presume most of them did). Church before seemed like a boring place, stuck in seemingly irrelevant tradition, where its fidgety youth just daydreamed through the service waiting for its last prayer to be over. How to reach out to them before they left to college and abandoned church altogether? Or how to bring back those who already had?

It is reported that the founder of the largest church in the Chicago area had a poster outside his office that read, "What is our business? Who is our costumer? What does the costumer consider value?"[7] If the American youth had lost focus on church due to their consumer-driven instant-gratifying habits, it was time to market to them as consumers. And what do young consumers want? Hip music sung by good-looking vocalists and guitarists, motivation to improve their lives in some way, and socializing with the right crowd. The megachurch delivered and it delivered well.

Did it work? Phenomenally well in many respects. Churches that used this strategy grew rapidly from just a few members to thousands, and sometimes tens of thousands. Surely those that attend these churches would feel confusion at the report that Christians are shrinking because that is not their immediate empirical evidence. So if some churches grew massively, it must have been at the expense of smaller congregations, not so much by the gaining of new converts as many would have desired. Sociologist of religion Mark Chavez confirms this trend of Christians moving from smaller to larger congregations.[8] Moreover, it is not very clear to what extent very large churches contribute to believers growing in the Christian virtues. The largest church in the Chicago area did a study of its own congregation and discovered that its most satisfied members were those who were in the initiation stages of Christianity. On the other hand, their most dissatisfied group was composed of generally committed members who were looking for "more in-depth teaching, more connection opportunities, [and] more serving options."[9] Chavez also confirms a similar trend in that those in larger congregations generally give less money and are less involved in the church's life.[10]

It is tempting to those who attend smaller congregations to scoff at the larger ones as market/consumer-driven corporations. But I don't think a specific congregation size is the solution to the problems that the church faces today. We shouldn't be too quick to judge as there are genuine benefits one can acquire from larger churches. For one, they do offer numerous programs throughout the week to meet the differing needs of its congregants. A college-aged small group will have different struggles from a middle-aged small group. Besides, some of these churches grew rapidly simply because their preaching was genuinely better. Moreover, a larger and more techie building may not be so much a reflection of misguided priorities, but rather a reflection of the financial efficiencies built into their larger system. I will argue later that if the church is in part constrained by lack of resources, there is a lot to learn from the more financially efficient congregations, many of which are the larger ones.

Sometimes as a reaction to larger churches, in more recent years there have been other experiments that push the envelope even further. To truly reach out to the unchurched, some have been congregating in pubs. Clearly any traditional liturgy would give way to a more informal casual ambience in these places.[11] Others have formed intentional communities in neglected urban areas in which members live together or in proximity within the neighborhood, often sharing a portion of their possessions. This has been characterized as the New Monasticism as members are inspired by the ancient traditions of clustered communities.[12] Some of these churches offer numerous programs for its members to be involved in during the week. Whether be it feeding the hungry, tutoring at-risk children in the neighborhood, or expressing faith through yoga or the visual arts, there is a wide variety of activities during the week for congregants to be involved in. These are all commendable works that witness to the political and economic nature of the church. Yet one still has to keep in mind that most of these activities take place in people's spare time, that is, after their work is over in a given day. One is still left to figure out how one's full-time job is related to the church. Besides, not everyone could possibly be fully involved in these activities, especially families with young children, as they already have too much on their plate. Though I have deep admiration for New Monasticism as a whole, I'm curious as to how sustainable it is for people to be committed to them in the long term. I wonder what their attrition rate is as some of their members eventually get married and have children. Not that everyone should be married, of course. After all, most monks and nuns did not. But I suspect that many young people that are part of the movement probably hope to form a family in the near future.

Pastors left and right, of both large and small congregations, often think that the solution to all our problems is simply to be more about the gospel or more loving. Who would disagree with that? The only problem is that there seems to be little agreement on what those terms mean. Myriads of books have been written on those topics and yet the church is still in decline. One has to keep in mind that the fastest shrinking congregations are those of the mainline Protestant denominations. Many of them have adopted a more liberal stance on homosexual marriage as a way of practicing inclusive love. One would think that the wider their doors, the more the people would come in, but ironically people have been running out through those wide doors instead. The mainline denominations shrank from 18.1 percent as a share of U.S. population in 2007 to 14.7 percent in 2014, the largest percentage decline of all major Christian groups.[13] It's to the extent that *New York Times* columnist Ross Douthat wrote an Easter piece titled "Save the Mainline," in which he proposed that the newspaper's liberal secular readers go back to the mainline churches from which they or their ideals originated. He also made the astute observation that the reason for the decline in liberal congregations is that what they offer is already embodied in mainstream liberal politics and culture, so why would anyone even bother attending church?[14]

In short, no amount of gimmicks from conservative and liberal, large and small churches is stemming the exodus. To be clear, I do not think that shrinking numbership is the main problem, but it is a symptom of a much larger sickness ailing the church. It is revealing that, contrary to the shrinking trend, polarization of conservatives and liberals has very visibly risen inside and outside of the church, as mentioned before. Perhaps the divisive 2016 elections had something to do with that, but I think the roots of the problem go down way deeper.

"IT'S THE ECONOMY, STUPID"— AND ALSO POLITICS

Douthat's piece offers clues as to what is ailing the church overall, not just the mainline. Is it bad that people have more interest in American politics than the church, regardless of whether they fall on the left or the right? Why should they not? After all, politics is about determining what the goods are that we have in common and how to produce and distribute them. These are not just identity and cultural goods but also material goods, which means that our politics is closely tied to our economics, and if so, it is also tied to our jobs and families. So why did liberals stop attending church, yet still attend Bernie Sanders rallies with a passion? Why were Trump rallies filled with more numbers and more energy than church? The basic answer is that there is something tangible at stake in what America offers, but not so much in the life of the church today. After all, who makes sure that justice, healthcare, education, welfare and jobs are provided for? Does the church do that? There was a time that it did. But now the nation-state, America, is the primary holder and distributor of those goods.

So what does the church do now exactly? I suppose it is in the business of saving souls. Because salvation has come to be understood by many Christians as merely making it to heaven, it has become very personal and individual business. The church then seems to have caved in to deal only with private matters such as personal morality, but shied away from public affairs. Does that leave it with anything to provide for on this side of the resurrection? Sure it does, but to put it bluntly, the church has basically been relegated to providing a social club for like-minded people to hang out with, and to providing therapy—making us feel better about our lives and relationships by improving them in some way. That's what we get for one or two hours on a Sunday. So why would anyone who has their life put together and has friends feel the need to attend church?

Therapy and friendships are of course of indispensable value and I do not mean to belittle the church's work today. That the church mostly provides these two goods is obviously a generalization, albeit a true one for many churches. And even if the church only offered these two goods, people should still attend. I do not use the word "therapy" here in a derogatory way. We should remember that Jesus came for the sick, not for those who proudly presume they are well (Luke 5.31). Society would be better off if all of us humbly recognized that we are sick in some way and we sought out help. For instance, I'm sure the church has saved many a flailing marriage. Besides, we should stop pretending that we have as many meaningful friendships as our Facebook pages feign. Loneliness is a real sickness ailing the individualistic West. It has gotten to the point that the British government recently appointed a Minister for Loneliness. But even if friendships and therapy are invaluable, doesn't all of this leave people craving for something more from the church?

Overall, the real problem is that the church has ceded all political and economic matters to the state. This has taken place over the last four hundred years with the rise of the nation-state. Because it happened generations ago, we have just taken it for granted that church today is what church is supposed to be, failing to notice that that wasn't always the case. Because the passing of time throughout history often gives the illusion of progress, I understand that many would argue that the current state of affairs is the way things should be. After all, the church should not be involved in matters of national defense. Nor should it force a specific religion on its citizens. The First Amendment correctly separates church and state. And, of course, the Crusades were a bad idea. But I'm just not so sure that that should make the church merely into a private country club. Nor am I sure that economic matters should be divorced from church. After all, the Bible is replete with economic talk from beginning to end. The kind of work people did and how they spent the fruit of their labor mattered to the temple and the church. Yet finances somehow became personal finances in America, where people think they have the right to spend their money they so arduously earned in whichever way they want.

In the process of the nation-state taking over these roles, America became the Savior, not Christ through the church. We Christians in America would like to think that we put God above any other. Anything less would smack of idolatry. But our practical lives reflect that we live as Americans first and Christians second. Consider the 2016 elections. About 80 percent of White evangelicals voted for Trump. Now why would evangelicals do that given that Trump's lifestyle is anything but Christian? Was it because he was against abortion and taxes? Perhaps in part, but how to explain that the percentage of evangelical voters was lower for George W. Bush when he also stood against abortion and taxes?[15] The excitement for Trump compared to previous Republican candidates was clearly palpable in his rallies, and it was obviously not for the abortion or tax issue. No. Trump's rallying cry was to "Make America Great Again."

To those on the left who despise Trump and his supporters as deplorables, they have to admit that many of the issues he campaigned for did stand for recovering America's place in the world, even if promises were not always kept. Does a nation need secure borders to keep its safety and sense of identity? Had American jobs bled for decades due to outsourcing and trade imbalances? Was the Obama administration's foreign policy somewhat unassertive? If one were to take a nationalist standpoint, the answer is yes indeed to all of the above.

While I had voted for Obama in 2008, I have to confess that, because part of me is American, while standing in front of the ballot in 2016, I was for a moment tempted to vote for Trump, but couldn't get myself to do it at the end. I walked out of the booth leaving the ballot empty. I hope that this doesn't make me deplorable to many a reader.

Yet it is precisely the nationalism of Donald Trump and his supporters that is problematic. The failure of so many of us Christians to see an issue here goes to show the extent to which, deep inside, we care more about America and its values than the church and its values. We must now live with the fact that we put someone in power that put our own protection first at the expense of Syrians as they were brutally massacred in their own country. And all this while the Scripture says, "Cursed be anyone who deprives the alien, the orphan, and the widow of justice" (Deut 27:19). We must live with the fact that we made a role model for our children out of someone that boasted of grabbing women by the genitals, just because we thought it was worth it to protect our comfortable way of life.

But is it really any surprise that we have done this given that it is America that provides us with protection, healthcare, education, welfare and justice? We Americans, Christians included, are anxious of losing our comfortable way of life, which was provided by no other than America. Because that way of life directly affects the welfare of our families, many valiant soldiers are willing to make the ultimate sacrifice for their nation. But would they also be willing to be martyrs for Christ and his church? Did the church provide any of our lifestyle? Perhaps only a small portion of it, indirectly. We therefore live, die, and vote as Americans first, Christians second. We are thus content to attend a church once a week that merely makes us feel a little better, gives us a little motivation to improve our personal lives, provides a safe community for our children, and licenses and sometimes encourages us to live as Americans for the rest of the week. That there were numerous Christians unfriending each other due to differing political allegiances goes to show where our true loyalties really are. The church should be a place of communion, but we have allowed our very American political loyalties to get in the way.

WHERE HOME IS

In this book I will argue that, at least for us Christians, *the church is and should be our true body politic, not the nation-state.* To think along these lines is what I believe will truly make us live as Christians first and Americans second, not the other way around. I do not claim that this is a novel idea in any way. I will argue that from the biblical text and from church history it is evident that the people of Israel and later Jesus Christ and his church were political through and through. Why else would anyone have crucified Jesus or persecuted the church? People don't often get killed for providing therapy and a little friendship. But people die, often times willingly, for political reasons as many a valiant soldier does for their nation.

A couple of political theologians have also prodded my thoughts in this direction. I am particularly indebted to professors Stanley Hauerwas and William Cavanaugh. Their work is at the forefront of exposing us to a much-needed robust understanding of what the church is and should be. Some of their maxims are worth mentioning in detail here.

Hauerwas has such a high view of the church that he says it "stands as a political alternative to every nation,"[16] that it is in itself "a social ethic."[17] But because the nation-state and other institutions have far surpassed the church in day-to-day relevance, part of the problem of the church is that it has tried to simply follow along what those institutions do and thus show that it too has some form of social ethic. So, for instance, when the state claims to provides equality and justice, the church tries to play catch-up like a child blurting out, "Me too! Me too! We support justice and equality too!" And so Christians end up doing the same things that the state does in the name of justice and equality. But then it is not at all clear why the church was needed in the first place. Hauerwas's project has been to let the church speak on its own terms. So instead of having Christians simply follow the state and other institutions, he is all about letting the church define first what concepts such as equality and justice truly mean in the light of God's truth, and then proceed from there. After all, the secular state or other institutions may be misguided in what they mean with justice and equality.

Because this requires that the church be a politics, Hauerwas says that the church is not "any less a human community than other forms of human association. As with other institutions, the church draws on and requires patterns of authority that derive from human needs for status, belonging, and direction."[18] What this means in practice is that, like other institutions, the church also has a hierarchy and as such it has authority to discipline its members. After all, if the church is to be called a holy people, "the church must vigorously attend to mutual upbuilding and correction."[19] I wonder how well that would sit with the many "nones" today, especially the "spiritual but not religious" type. Such people have been sharply on the rise, even among those who profess to be Christian.[20] Often what they mean is that they are fed up with organized religion, its abuse of authority, its corruption, its bureaucracy. The church has abused its authority countless times, no doubt. But to altogether throw away the institutional character of the church is a very individualistic and thus a distinctly Western move.

Of course, Hauerwas is also famous for the dictum that modernity produced "people who believe they should have no story except the story they choose when they have no story."[21] Americans in particular are a people who like to believe in the story of self-sufficiency. We like to say that we pulled ourselves up by our bootstraps and made it on our own. We want freedom from just about everything, which means also that we do not want to be bound to anyone, whether they be our parents, our boss, or our organized religion–like church. And given our divorce rates, we apparently want freedom from our spouses too.

Yet I wonder whether those who despise organized religion would readily quit their company they work for or even give up their nationality. Of course some would, only to take up another job at another corporation or pick up another nationality. The point here is that a nation or a corporation is in many ways like an "organized religion." They have their own bureaucracy, budgets, flags, logos, chants, and so on. So isn't it something that people are willing to submit to their nation or their company, but not their church? Christians are supposed to be a people that submit to the church, yet the church is unable to discipline its people because members are free to leave at any given time. What is the church supposed to do when people have an attitude like, "I'll just go to the church next block if I don't like your sermon"? In the consumerist culture that we live in, churches often compete for members as though they were customers and will therefore shape their worship in a way that pleases their congregants. We claim to be free, even from the church and its correction, yet we are a lonely bunch that yearns for deeper community and belonging. We have to come to the realization that we can't have it both ways. Any marriage counselor would tell us that.

As for William Cavanaugh, he is someone who studied under Hauerwas and has therefore congenial views. He has taken it upon himself to explore in more detail the rise of the nation-state and what the church's response has been and should be. The extent to which the state has claimed our imagination is well illustrated in Cavanaugh's opening paragraph in *Theopolitical Imagination*:

> How does a provincial farm boy become persuaded that he must travel as a soldier to another part of the world and kill people he

> knows nothing about? He must be convinced of the reality of borders, and imagine himself deeply, mystically, united to a wider national community that stops abruptly at those borders.[22]

There is a sense in which the nation is real, and yet at the same time it's not. It's like money in that sense, which, by the way, is printed by the state. Money only has value so far as we have faith in it. That's why when people lose faith in the economy, it crashes. In the same way, there is something real about the armies, the bureaucracy, and the borders of the nation. Yet in some ways, it was all just the product of someone's imagination—the borders that someone drew and the Constitution that someone drafted—and our willingness to buy into it.

As far as denominational lines go, Cavanaugh is a Catholic while Hauerwas has often called himself an "ecclesial whore," jumping from church to church, mostly in the Protestant tradition. As for me, I am an evangelical. I hope that this shows that their ideas and mine should be thoroughly ecumenical in character. In the polarized times that we live in, the most significant division within the church has become that between liberals and conservatives, which crosses all denominational lines. The "conservative" and "liberal" categories as used in our times seem to be based on disagreements on what is best for the nation. That means that there is an underlying assumption that the nation is our true polis, which makes it all the more urgent to come together and recover the sense that the church is our true politics.

If Hauerwas and Cavanaugh have done a pretty good job in expounding on the thesis above, why then is this book needed? Some say that Hauerwas is someone that needs no introduction. He was after all named in 2001 as the best theologian in America by *Time* magazine. But the reality is that I have been in and out of several Christian circles in which the name Hauerwas doesn't ring a bell. Anyone who says that Hauerwas needs no introduction has been too close in proximity to the ivory towers, and not sufficiently grounded in the real world. Hauerwas and Cavanaugh have tried to make their work accessible, but because they reside in academia, their own attempts have not been sufficient. Moreover, though Hauerwas is a great theologian, when it comes to practical issues, he has mostly dealt with issues pertaining peace and war, medical ethics, and disability. He hasn't really offered concrete economic solutions. Cavanaugh is the one who has taken on that task. But Cavanaugh seems to tackle the economic issue mostly from a consumer perspective—demonstrating how we can faithfully make consumer choices—but not sufficiently from the producer's perspective—how an economy can produce meaningful jobs, where we spend forty to eighty hours of our weekly lives.[23] Addressing the second problem is harder, as it would require a thorough reimagination and reorganization of society. Ultimately, most of us are fortunate enough not to face war or medical dilemmas in our everyday choices, but it is our jobs that eat up the vast majority of our lives, so this is a crucial matter. It is my intention to do so in this book in the most accessible way possible.

Solutions are certainly not easy to come up with, let alone implement, but there is a lot at stake here. If we truly lived as though we are Christians first and Americans second, the current polarization would not be splitting Christians apart. The church is a catholic body and should behave as such, which means that it crosses all national, ethnic, gender, and socioeconomic boundaries. Second, all facets of our lives would be more properly integrated under the church. Moral values, our families, the economy, school, our jobs, and business would not seem so fractured from each other. Where we spend forty to eighty hours a week should be imbued with purpose, community, and discipline that leads to Christian character. The church loses members not because there is anything egregiously wrong with its worship services (although that may be the case for a few), but because the church touches Christians for only one or two hours a week. All gimmicks tried by churches on the left and right have been for the most part a reorganization of those few hours. At the end of the day, providing hip music, better sermons, and greasier pizza for the youth, all just for a couple hours a week, cannot possibly compete with the entertainment that the Internet offers; the community, purpose, and discipline that a corporation offers; or the liberal or conservative values that the Democratic and Republican parties stand for. Is it any wonder that the church is shrinking? I do not want to be misunderstood here. I am not arguing for more church time with more burdensome church programs throughout the week that people barely have the time for. No. As it will be clear, I will be arguing for a reimagination and restructuring of society in which the church is politically involved in all facets of our lives.

This book then is a summons to all thoughtful Christians who sense there is something wrong—whether it be laity or church leaders of all denominations, conservatives and liberals, young and old, of means and without means—to pull our resources together, whatever they may be, to reimagine and restructure society so we can have church in the proper sense once again. This does not necessarily call for leaving one's local church for another, but to build it up by reimagining one's own. If Jesus is Lord, he must be Lord of every aspect of our lives, not just a couple hours of our week. Once we have placed our family, politics, economics, and our jobs under Jesus' feet, I suspect we will then discover what it really means to live in community with each other, which is what the church should be. This community should be so otherworldly that one should clearly be able to tell a Christian from a non-Christian.

People often talk about having a longing for deep community, which they often fail to find in the church. A lot of churches give the impression that community is all about hanging out and having a good time. This is what "love" or "the gospel" has been watered down to. So newcomers of a church often go through an exciting phase of getting to know and being known by others, and then as time goes by it all fizzles down. Is it any surprise that those of us who are not too sociable have a hard time finding a role in a church? But I would say that *a true community is one where its members have political and economic commitments to each other,* at least to some degree. That was the case with the people of Israel and in the early church. If the church truly embodied love and the gospel—if they loved each other politically and economically—then why would anyone leave the church? Let us then embark on this adventurous journey together.

2.

How We Got Here

The Rise of the State

So how is it that the church today has been relegated to the role of therapist and party planner? How is it that the nation-state became the locus of our politics, taking on almost every other conceivable serious role? How is it that corporations took over economic matters? And how is it that our lives are so fractured that we do not know how to make sense of each part in relation to another? All of these questions are related and multiple answers from various angles could be provided. The short answer is that in the past the church was a unified politics, albeit imperfectly. The church provided a unified worldview that related all aspects of life to itself. But with the rise of the secular nation-state (e.g., America), the state slowly took over every serious role the church had. Most states claim religious impartiality, so everything the state put its hands on also became non-religious, thereby fracturing the various facets of life which the church had once held together.

Many readers may think that all of this has been for the better. Perhaps that is true in some ways. But we should not simply take our present situation as a given without competing alternatives. After all, many ancient societies were organized differently. Some were confederations—small sovereign city-states loosely unified—while others were tribes unified mostly by kin, and still others theocracies ruled by priests. Why do we naturally assume that our present state of affairs is the best we've had? Is it because we think that history moves humanity forward through time? That has certainly not always been the case. Besides, the nation-state itself did not always have the noblest of beginnings, as we will explore in this chapter.

THE WARS OF RELIGION

In a four-hundred-page volume, historian Brad Gregory tries to tackle the issue of why the various facets of our lives became so fractured. In *The Unintended Reformation*, his thesis is that it all started with the Protestant Reformation, as his title explicitly states. Now this may sound too bold for Protestants and evangelicals to swallow. After all, wasn't the Protestant Reformation necessary to counter the corruption of the Catholic Church—to halt the sale of indulgences and the excesses of Renaissance popes? Didn't the Reformation recover "the gospel"—that we are saved only by the grace of God? Didn't it give us Bible-centered churches vibrant with committed Christians? Maybe. But I would advise the reader who answers "yes" to all of the above not to jettison all of Gregory's argument simply because his thesis seems a tad offensive. The sweeping thesis may at times sound unconvincing, but in many of the details, I think Gregory correctly traces the evolution of various strands of ideas and their connections. Besides, Gregory is not concerned with attacking Reformation leaders and their supporters. He says in the title of his book itself that whatever the outcome, it was *unintended*, in other words, that these were side-effects of a movement, even if it had noble intentions. I have found no other work that addresses the fragmentation of the various facets of our lives as thoroughly as Gregory's. Each chapter of his work is about one aspect of our life that has been pulled asunder from religious faith in the West.

Gregory states that because of the rise of the nation-state, "whether in Western confessional, liberal, or totalitarian regimes, states control churches: whether they prescribe, permit, or proscribe religion, they do so entirely on their terms, exercising an institutional monopoly of power in the public sphere."[24] We usually think that it is totalitarian states like communist China or North Korea that control religion. But liberal democracies controlling religion? On the surface it may not seem so, but we have to ask ourselves, ultimately, who is subservient to whom? Upon careful examination, we would find that religious organizations always have to play by the rules of the state. For instance, can public school teachers teach from their personal religious worldview? Or can churches protect some of its members from deportation?

What then led to the rise of the modern nation-state? To start with, we have to admit that the Protestant Reformation wrought not just religious, but also political divisions in Europe on an unprecedented scale. What used to be a unified Catholic Europe was suddenly divided between Catholic and Protestant states. Notice I said "states," not "churches." The Reformation was not just a cordial religious debate among churches, but a deeply political conflict among states. For instance, the Reformer Martin Luther and his ideas would not have gained prominence, let alone survived, had he not received shelter and support from several German princes (heads of states). So was the case with other Reformers. Why else were the Lutherans, the Reformed, and the Church of England among the groups that had lasting political consequence in contrast to other Protestant groups such as the Anabaptists, Munsterites, Mennonites, and Hutterites? Is it really because the former's ideas were truer than the latter's? Not really. The reason is simply because the former three enjoyed the political approval and support of powerful secular states in contrast to the latter groups, which were often persecuted not just by the Roman church but also by secular states.[25]

Because Luther knew so well that he needed political support, he even wrote a letter titled *To the Christian Nobility of the German Nation*, in which he went as far as to charm the German princes by proposing that no taxes be paid to the Roman church and that no secular matters be referred to Rome.[26] Rulers had been bickering throughout most of the Middle Ages with the church in Rome over what areas they had jurisdiction on, so which ruler would not have agreed with Luther? And precisely because Luther needed the princes' support, he licensed them to crush their own rebelling peasants, calling them "faithless, perjured, disobedient, rebellious murderers, robbers, and blasphemous,"[27] and thus deserving of punishment, though the peasants themselves may have been influenced by Luther's ideas.

Europe then became politically divided between Protestants and Catholics. Violence soon erupted in what are known as the Wars of Religion, which devastated Europe for decades. Weary of it all, matters were finally settled in the Peace of Westphalia for Germany and the Edict of Nantes for France, both of which finally introduced the idea of tolerance in Europe. After all the bloodshed, it was pretty clear that Protestants and Catholics were not going to relent on their beliefs, so there was no other way to end the carnage but to learn to live with each other. The common narrative here is that the cooler heads of states had to intervene to put an end to the bloodshed caused by religious fanatics. For instance, those who came together to draft the Peace of Westphalia were the various state delegations.[28] The same could be said about the Edict of Nantes, of which the king of France was the main actor.[29] The state, as a non-religious and impartial third party, became the new savior, the grantor of peace between Protestants and Catholics, and thus rose in prominence above the warring churches.

There is certainly a lot of truth in this narrative. But we must be careful in choosing what lessons to draw from it. Does this violent period in history really teach us that a secular state is really less violent and therefore a better politics than a religious body? According to Cavanaugh, the Wars of Religion "were not events that necessitated the birth of the modern state . . . but were fought largely for the aggrandizement of the emerging state."[30] In other words, the state was not really needed as some form of savior to end the bloodshed. This is because the main actors of these wars were primarily motivated by their desire for more political power, rather than by their religious beliefs. To provide an example, Charles V, a Catholic ruler who waged war against Protestants, had actually sacked Catholic Rome first.[31] Or there was even a time when the Lutheran princes were aided by the Catholic King Henry II.[32] Could these moves have been motivated by religious zealotry? Each ruler obviously was merely seeking what was most beneficial to them in their position. Is it surprising then that it was the secular rulers who had to broker the peace? They had to fix what they were responsible for starting. The Wars of Religion are often used as an illustration of the damaging effects of religious zealotry. There is a lot of truth in that of course. But is zealotry for the state any better? Let's not forget that the most violent wars we've had were the two world wars, both of which were motivated by nationalism, the aggrandizing of the secular state.

LOYALTY TO TWO KINGDOMS?

In reviewing this brief history, it is important to note that the support that Luther received from German princes was not a merely circumstantial political accident. Luther could seek their support because of his deeply held political theology, which later became known as the two kingdoms doctrine. Luther believed that while on this Earth all of us belong to two kingdoms at the same time, one ruled by God and the other by the secular state. Each of these has its own realm, meaning that the church's jurisdiction became the saving of the soul while the state's jurisdiction became basically every other economic and political matter. Luther in particular emphasized Romans 13:1 to argue his case, which says, "Let every person be subject to the governing authorities; for there is no authority except from God, and those authorities that exist have been instituted by God."[33] Luther thought that if the state was instituted by God, then it must be respected by the church. The state is an agent of God to bring order in society, as is shown in the subsequent verse of Romans 13: "For the authority does not bear the sword in vain! It is the servant of God to execute wrath on the wrongdoer" (13:4). All of this should lend credence to the suggestion that it was in the Protestant Reformation that the seeds of the modern nation-state were laid.

It is easy to be seduced by this two kingdoms doctrine. Because of our current political circumstances, most Christians live by it even if they don't know or care much about Luther. It does seem to make sense in many respects. If the state can't act as a separate realm from the church, who else is going to establish justice and order in our society? Can the church really yield the sword? It would offend our sensibilities to do that as Christians, so we just let the state do the dirty work of national defense and policing our communities. All the while we worship peacefully in our churches and wash our hands of the violence of the state we supported.

I would like to point out here that those who are indignant of the violence of the medieval church while they allow the state to protect them now are being hypocritical. The church's violence during medieval times was a result of the church asserting political force in order to fill the power vacuum left by the fall of the Roman Empire. Because there was no other powerful state to fill in the void that Rome left, the church mistakenly took on the role of Rome, which was at times to establish order through force. To be clear, I do not in any way endorse here what the church did. Things like the Crusades were terrible ideas. But unlike today, back then the church saw itself as a politics, yet it erred in thinking that it had to mirror the violent politics that the Roman Empire left behind.

So where does that leave us now? I do not want to be misunderstood. Just because I say that the church should recover a sense that it is a politics doesn't mean that I am advocating here for the abolition of the secular state by the church. That would only be possible by means of a violent revolution, of which the church should have no business. A church that takes power by force would only repeat the violent politics of the Middle Ages. It would seem then that there is no other alternative but to live as though there are two separate kingdoms, at least in practice.

Does that mean that we simply move on with our lives as though there is no other alternative? No. What I am arguing in this book is in part what Hauerwas has pointed out—that the church should embody an "alternative politics." In *Resident Aliens*, Hauerwas compares the church to "a colony . . . a beachhead, an outpost, an island of one culture in the middle of another."[34] So even though it seems like we live in two kingdoms simultaneously, the church is and should be our true outpost. Ultimately our allegiance to the church should trump over our allegiance to the state by far. Of course, there are issues over which both the state and the church agree, but many over which they do not. Which one we follow in times of disagreement projects our true colors. To clarify here, issues of contention between both kingdoms are not limited to abstract ideals that only rouse discord at the dinner table. If the church is an outpost and the state is the wider world, this should not mean that each simply has a separate jurisdiction over various facets of life. It's not that the church's role should be simply the saving of souls while the state is left to deal with all political and economic matters. The fact is that there will be conflicts between church and state on many issues and we Christians have to keep our allegiances straight.

Yet many churches, in going along with Luther (whether they are aware of it or not), behave as though they have taken this separation of roles for granted. And so it is that there is hardly any conflict between the church and the state. The church in a sense has been co-opted by the state, becoming its right-hand man, ensuring that it raises good and moral citizens for the state. This political captivity of the church is our current state of affairs that must be addressed.

LET THERE BE LIGHT?

Let's go back to tracing the rise of the nation-state. Once nation-states started to gain power apart from the Catholic Church, all they were missing was a philosophical justification for their existence. That justification came in the movement known as the Enlightenment. One of its earliest thinkers was Thomas Hobbes, who famously said that when humans are in a state of nature without the state ruling over them, their lives are "solitary, poore, nasty, brutish and short."[35] Hobbes here is giving us his version of human origins and how and why government was instituted. Essentially he is saying that way in the past, before we were civilized and therefore had no government ruling over us, we were like boorish monkeys fighting for a limited number of bananas. With no authority to establish any form of order, only the strongest survived. One may think that the strongest would have really liked to live in this kind of a society, but according to Hobbes even the strongest have to "live in continuall feare, and danger of violent death."[36] This is because one usually does not get to keep the position of big bully for very long, for there is always someone else who comes and challenges his or her position. This is all very brutish indeed. Because nobody wants to live in continuous fear and danger of violent death, eventually people come together and form a *contract* with each other. In it, they renounce some of their freedoms and grant authority to a governing authority that will provide them order and peace. For this governing authority to accomplish its goal, it must be as strong as a *leviathan*, a term used to describe an ancient mythical monster, hence the name of Hobbes's work. This leviathan happens to be the modern nation-state.

It should be evident from here that there are clear points of departure of the Enlightenment from the Christian faith. Cavanaugh points out that the story laid out in the first chapters of Genesis is not one of humans living solitary, poor, nasty, brutish and short lives. Rather, human beings were created in God's image for communion with God and with one another. It is because of Adam's disobedience to God that this communion is fractured. If this is true, then unity is restored through participation in Christ's body, the new Adam, which is also the church, not merely in humans signing some contract among themselves.[37]

Though many subsequent Enlightenment philosophers did not share Hobbes's bleak view of human nature, they still managed to arrive to similar conclusions regarding the foundations of the state. Though Jean-Jacques Rousseau, in contrast to Hobbes, believed that humans behaved best in their natural state, he agreed with Hobbes that people eventually accede to being governed by making a *social contract*, hence the title of his work by that name.[38] Along this line of thought, John Locke later elaborated on the purpose of that government, stating that it is to protect man's inalienable rights of life, liberty, and property.[39] Another philosopher, Baron de Montesquieu, was inspired by the Roman republic and proposed a similar system of separation of powers to check and balance each other,[40] so the state would better serve the people. Though they all had differing ideas, most Enlightenment thinkers shared the view that the source of authority of governments was to be derived from the people. In all this, there was very little mention of God as the source of authority.

This doesn't mean that Enlightenment thinkers renounced Christian beliefs altogether. Even if some did, the influence of a prevalent Christian worldview is clearly present in some of their writings. This is most evident in Locke's case, for whom it would have been hopeless to argue that man has inalienable rights apart from him being created in the image of God.[41] How else would we be justified in saying that people have rights? There is no more convincing reason than the value given to humans by God as the foundation of rights. The nation-state then is the product of a concoction of various and sometimes contradicting ideals. Some of these ideals have echoes of the Christian faith, Roman government, and the belief in human reason and progress.

THE AMERICAN EXPERIMENT

The practice of Enlightenment ideals arrived in the experiment known as the United States. The founding documents of this country reveal an unmistakable appropriation of Enlightenment ideas. Take, for instance, the Constitution. The very first three words in the preamble say in large bold font, "We the People," making sure we would not miss who this document originated from. The preamble goes on to say the purpose: "in Order to form a more perfect Union . . . do ordain and establish this Constitution for the United States of America."[42] What else is this document but a *social contract* among the people? Or take the Declaration of Independence, whose famous words say that "all men . . . are endowed by their Creator with certain unalienable Rights, that among these are life, liberty, and the pursuit of happiness."[43] Thomas Jefferson took these words directly from John Locke, only changing "property" to "the pursuit of happiness." As for the system of separation of powers, it was clearly enshrined throughout the U.S. Constitution, giving us our president, our courts, and Congress.

So how did the experiment fare, given that it was based on a hodgepodge of various differing ideals? Initially, it seems to have gone quite well. America is indeed a great and noble nation, arguably the greatest of nations there has ever been in human history. Even before America became a global superpower, its life and institutions were greatly admired and people from all over the world sought to immigrate to it. As far back as the mid-1800s, Alexis de Tocqueville observed that the American people offered the best exemplar of an equal society.[44] It is worth noting here that de Tocqueville believed democracy worked well in America because its people were religious.[45] American democracy seemed to be such a success that the American Revolution and its Constitution were the inspiration in the formation of many other nation-states around the world. The freedoms provided by its institutions also encouraged entrepreneurship and industry, which in combination with its abundant natural resources made it into an economic powerhouse. The wealth created by industry lifted up the average person's standard of living significantly. From the development of the syphonic jet toilet to the sewing machine, industry blurred the lines between social classes by democratizing products that were once luxuries. For instance, by 1929, America produced five sixths of all cars in the world, providing one car for every five people in the country.[46]

People from all over the world were eager to come to the American shores, leaving behind family and even sometimes cultural ties as they sought to assimilate. The statue of liberty became a beacon of hope and salvation as immigrants poured in through Ellis Island. The famous inscription on the statue, which reads, "Give me your tired, your poor, Your huddled masses yearning to breathe free," rings true to many around the world. It is to be noted that America was and is special compared to other nations, in that many of its people believed that it was the ideals of liberty and equality that unified them, rather than a common ethnic background. It is this belief that has made America welcome numerous immigrants during the last century. America then became the ultimate meritocracy, a place that can boast that so many immigrants came to it destitute, yet "made it."

It is also this strong belief in liberty that made America the defender of democratic values all over the world. It fought German and Japanese oppressors during the Second World War. After victory, instead of taking revenge against its enemies, the U.S. aided Germany's and Japan's reconstruction by providing what today would be the equivalent of billions of dollars in loans to each. In doing so, it ensured that democracy would flourish on them and, as a result, today Japan and Germany are the world's third and fourth largest economies, respectively. America also made sure that communism would not spread and, as a consequence, countries like Germany and South Korea have benefited enormously from that. South Korea today is the twelfth largest economy in the world. Even under the Trump administration, America still provides tens of billions of dollars in global aid, far outpacing any other wealthy country. The U.S. does so in order to promote peace, development and disaster relief. Can anyone really deny America's magnanimous history?

Yet many readers would see that the above paragraphs make for too simplistic a history. The goal and scope of this book after all is not to delve into every detail of the history of the United States. Yet it is important to recognize that the American experiment came at the expense of many. The forced migration of Native Americans decimated their population from 120,000 in 1820 to fewer than 30,000 by 1844.[47] Words also cannot do justice to how brutal and racist American slavery was. The constant whippings, the sale of immediate family members, and the intentional withholding of education all attest to America's indelible national sin. All the while, women also did not always enjoy the same freedoms and privileges as men did. They only received the right to vote a century ago, in 1919. As to foreign affairs, America's involvement in the world is riddled with moral ambiguities, as is the case with the wars with Mexico, Vietnam, and Iraq. In the Mexican-American War, to put it simply, the United States took by sheer force half of the territory that belonged to another sovereign nation. Out of fear that the Vietnamese would choose communism, the United States supported a dictator who blocked democratic elections again and again. And even if one were to accept that America's hegemony has had salubrious effects overall, America's place in the world is currently threatened by the rise of Russia and China.

As for the standard of living provided by its economic institutions, the outcome still remains to be seen. The financial collapse of 2008 revealed that America's economic institutions are not as solid as we once thought they were. We are coming to the realization that the "free" market cannot be left completely to itself. It almost seems as though communist China is doing better at regulating its market. Moreover, the gap between the haves and the have-nots continues to grow with no end in sight. Medicare and the Social Security seem on the brink of collapse as politicians do not find it in their best interest to fix them. All the while, the polarization is so extreme that there is hardly any discourse that is civil from both sides of the aisle. It's to the extent that many pundits have expressed concern for the future of democracy.

At the end of the day, a nation founded on vague non-religious concepts of liberty and equality will come to be fractured. If there is no religious or moral framework, what is liberty after all? It becomes merely the ability to do as one pleases without infringing on someone else's liberty. For many Americans liberty has just become the freedom to make and spend money, which is another way to say that they have become slaves to their possessions. We are desiring creatures, after all, and something or someone will always take a hold of our hearts and minds. And how noble is the American meritocracy if society incentivizes one to use one's merit for money? If money and the individualistic lifestyle that comes with it is our unifying factor, how much longer will this experiment last? How long can the United States really remain united? As it turns out, we are starting to see the fractures right now.

Christians are not supposed to be a people with anxiety about America's decline. After all, every empire throughout human history has risen and fallen, yet the kingdom of God remains. Yet Trump's electoral victory reveals that Christians are indeed anxious. This anxiety arises from presupposing the nation-state as protector and guarantor of our freedoms, rights, and ultimately our way of life. But it is precisely this lack of political imagination that gave us some of those moral ambiguities that haunt us throughout America's history.

It should not be surprising that America's rise as a global superpower in the twentieth century coincided with the rise of Reinhold Niebuhr as America's theologian. Just as Billy Graham was America's pastor because of his frequent presence at the White House, Niebuhr was America's theologian as he frequented State Department meetings, especially during the Cold War. He became a favorite of Jimmy Carter, Barack Obama, and lately James Comey, to mention a few. Just like Luther, Niebuhr made a distinction between applying Jesus' precepts in our personal lives and applying them to a nation as a whole. He didn't think one could apply Jesus' precepts collectively as a nation. As an individual, you can be a good Christian by turning the other cheek when someone smacks you. But can a nation really do that? It wouldn't survive if it did so. Moreover, Niebuhr would have asked whether we are really practicing the command to love if we don't act forcefully to stop the horrors of the likes of Stalin and Hitler.[48] Niebuhr does sound very reasonable here. How else are we to survive and protect human rights all across the world? But what is troubling is that since Niebuhr was concerned mostly with America's role in global affairs, he makes little mention about the church's role in America or our lives.[49] It's as though the church is an afterthought for him. Yet this is precisely our same problem today, that the state has supplanted the church in our political and therefore moral imagination.

THE CURIOUS CASE OF GERMANY

What are the dangers of letting the state supplant the church in our political imagination? The case of Nazi Germany provides a case in point. I mention the Nazis here not because I think America is in any way as evil. But extreme examples are helpful as they can shed light on where an idea can lead if it is pursued all the way to its conclusion. What do we find when we examine Germany's case? Adolf Hitler is known as the main culprit of the horrors of Nazi Germany, but we should never forget that the Nazi Party came to power democratically elected by the people.[50] So what exactly led to Nazi popularity? Were the German people really such an evil bunch? Some would argue so. But then again, we should keep in mind that there is evil in all of us and, if given the proper (or improper) circumstances, we are all capable of it.

After Germany came out on the losing side of the First World War, it had no choice but to accept the terms of the treaty that ended the war, the Treaty of Versailles. Harsh would be an understatement to describe the terms it laid against Germany. Germany was to accept the sole guilt for the war and was therefore to make $32 billion in reparations to the Allies,[51] an impossible sum to pay at the time. Germany was also to surrender all of its colonies and the size of its army was to be kept at a bare minimum. A people that produced the likes of Brahms, Beethoven, Kant, and Hegel was suddenly brought down to its knees. Because it became impossible to repay its war debt, the government had to resort to printing vast amounts of money, which in turn led to hyperinflation. To see the scale of it, in October of 1923, one kilo of rye bread cost 5.5 billion marks. Just a month later it cost 428 billion marks.[52] To put this into perspective, imagine that you were a prudent German who had saved up enough to buy a house. As it turns out, a month later you wouldn't be able to buy even a used car with it. Wealth held in cash was totally obliterated. If the 2008 recession was painful to Americans, the early 1920s must have been living hell for Germans. Then along came Adolf Hitler, who in repudiation to the Treaty of Versailles propped up the German economy and military. This not only meant that more men would be recruited into the army, but also that the economy would be propped up with much-needed jobs in ammunition factories.[53] To put it bluntly, Hitler was all about Making Germany Great Again. After the utter humiliation that the Germans had suffered, who among them wouldn't love Hitler? It's easy for us to pass judgment on the

Germans in retrospect, but before the war started who would have known he would turn out to be a monster?

What is truly disturbing in all of this history is that about 95 percent of Germans were Christians at the time.[54] Are we to say that they were all fake Christians? Surely many of them must have been sincere believers. But then why didn't the German church stand up to the Nazis? How were they so easily duped into being collaborators? The sad reality is that many theologians, those who led the church, enthusiastically supported Hitler. For instance, Paul Althaus, who welcomed Hitler's chancellorship as a "miracle of God," appreciated Nazi law and order, as he stated that "punishment shall again be taken seriously as retribution."[55] One can see echoes of Luther's two kingdoms doctrine here. The state is entrusted by God to yield the sword to provide law and order. Althaus was, after all, a Luther scholar. Another theologian, by the name of Emanuel Hirsch, believed that God meets humanity through their Volk, their people, their fatherland. He also believed in Hegelian fashion that God was the God of history, leading its continual progress, but that his great Volk had been humiliated through the Treaty of Versailles.[56] To put it another way, many Christians at that time believed that the Christian faith should advance culture and civilization forward. Why would God be against the flourishing and advancement of humanity and its culture, after all? It so happens that Germany had been a cultured and industrious civilization whose development had been suddenly arrested by the Treaty of Versailles. Therefore it was not only acceptable but also imperative for church leaders to support a leader that repudiated Versailles, namely, Hitler.

I hope here not to offend the reader with Republican leanings. On certain issues, I can count myself as one after all. I do not mean to say that Donald Trump is comparable in character to Adolf Hitler. That would be an unfair mischaracterization. Despite his numerous flaws, Trump is obviously an incomparably better person than Hitler was. That I need to take the time here to make this clarification goes to show the polarized times we live in. Yet I hope to make it evident that there are some parallels between America now and Germany then, if not between their leaders. The leaders merely reflect the people's wishes.

Both Hitler and Trump came to power at a time when the wounds of an economic calamity were still fresh. They both campaigned on restoring the greatness of their nation at a time when both nations' place in the world was in decline. As a result, during his speeches, Hitler was vitriolic against Jews and anyone whom he thought diminished his nation's greatness. Trump and his supporters have also been chastised by the media for their vitriol against illegal immigration. To be fair, it's not even Trump, but his supporters he energizes, that are the worst offenders. On an appearance she made in a college campus, Ann Coulter said that she was "totally a 'looksist'" and could determine who should be allowed into the country just by looking at their physical appearance.[57] Was that just too low and vulgar? Certainly. Yet why are we so shocked by her words? After all, nation-states are by definition enclosed within a territory and therefore have borders that determine the limits of their sovereignty. As such, they have always made a distinction between their citizens from *others*. The otherness of those that are outside the boundaries of a nation is fabricated by definition in the polity that is the nation-state. And who wouldn't want to assemble only the cream of the crop in their nation?

What we are witnessing in the likes of Trump and Coulter is merely the true colors of this powerfully seductive idea called nationalism. Previous presidents and public servants restrained themselves from going down the deep end under the guise of political correctness. But with a president that does not care to offend, it should be evident where nationalism leads when pursued to its practical conclusion. I guess we can thank Trump and Coulter for making that crystal clear. Is their vulgar anti-immigration rhetoric really that different from Hitler's anti-Semitic rants? After all, during his early speeches no one suspected that that would eventually lead to the Holocaust. The only difference is that the United States is mostly concerned with potential immigrants outside of its borders whereas Germany was concerned with Jews already living within its borders. For that, we could never expect Trump to be as violent as Hitler was. It is not my hope here to paint all these leaders as monsters. They are or were merely human, just like the rest of us, and perhaps all too human. It just goes to show the powerful hold that nationalism as an idea can have in a people's imagination.

DO DEMOCRATS OR REPUBLICANS HAVE THE ANSWER?

There has certainly been a barrage of criticism towards Trump by the left-leaning media. But are liberals really that different from conservatives? Do they hold some hallowed higher ground? To start with, the rhetoric used in reaction to Trump's victory revealed that liberals are not necessarily the loving, inclusive, and tolerant bunch they claim to be. What can we say of people in the leftist media posing for a photo with a replica of Trump's decapitated head, or worse, mocking Trump's then eleven-year-old son on social media? How many laughs did they get? Where has civility gone today?

In today's polarized climate, people have the illusion that one party stands for something while the other stands for completely the opposite view. But politicians play the game of giving us amnesia, and they play it very well. Because Trump's platform was big on building a wall, and because Democratic politicians find it convenient to react strongly to it, people tend to think that only Republicans are interested in curtailing immigration. The reality is that even Bernie Sanders is against open borders. It was even posted on his website until he found it convenient to take that page down.[58] Of course not many noticed it because the entry was written in 2015, one year before Trump came into the spotlight. Besides, people forget that President Obama was derided by some as "deporter-in-chief," as five million undocumented immigrants were deported under his watch.[59] Trump criticized Obama for being weak on immigration, but in some ways Obama was actually tougher. It's ironic how Trump got the heat for his immigration policies and yet he takes pride on that, even though it's based on lies. The bizarre world of politics we live in!

As for liberals who don't hold public office, many are a rather conflicted bunch I think. On the one hand, some love their nation dearly and claim to do all the lefty stuff they do for the sake of their nation. Yet they fail to discern the kind of polity where their ideals would be most at home. Are their ideals really reconcilable with the kind of polity that the nation-state is and was meant to be? I suppose only some of these ideals are. For the sake of consistency, even someone like Bernie Sanders had to stand against open borders. At the end of the day, his primary polity is the nation-state, which by definition needs borders. Besides, because ideals such as liberty and equality remain vague when taken from their religious context, the final result is the fracturing of society. Let's admit that Douthat was right in his *Times* piece in saying that liberals should go back to church, where many of their ideals originated. After all, the church is the true catholic polity without boundaries, where people of every nation and race, where the most oppressed and marginalized are welcome, not just to be given the freedom simply to make money, but to have communion with God and with one another.

But one can see why liberals identified the nation-state as their primary polity while abandoning the church. Obviously there are numerous reasons combined, but Douthat pointed out that it was the Democratic Party that came to truly embody liberal politics. After all, the Democratic Party is part of national politics, where the weightier matters of economics, healthcare, welfare, and education are discussed and resolved. In contrast, to what extent can the church embody any politics when it is mostly a social club that meets a couple hours a week? Why would anyone feel like the church has any relevance?

If one really thinks about it, Republicans and Democrats are just two sides of the same coin. They both operate under the assumption that the nation-state is the locus of all meaningful political and economic discourse and practice. I have attempted to succinctly narrate in this chapter how that came to be. That Christians fiercely cling to either party goes to show that they have lost all political imagination. Like I said, we claim to be Christians, but we live as Americans first, Christians second. We expect the state to be the savior; to provide, regulate, and distribute justice, healthcare, welfare, education, protection. But we have no such expectation from the church. The telltale sign is that we consider it more important who our president is than who our pastor is. After all, the pastor is merely a counselor for when we are feeling depressed or when our marriages are falling apart. So we have entrusted the state with more and more powers over time. We even want the state to provide solutions to our increasing drug overdose and suicide epidemics, issues that were normally considered to fall under the jurisdiction of therapists and the church.

It is in the process of allotting more powers to the state that our lives became fractured to the extent that we are unable to make sense of how economics, family, work, faith, and education have any bearing with each other. The state claims to be a purely non-religious and thus morally neutral agent. So why would the state imbue any of these facets of life that it regulates with moral values? As a result, economics has become a discipline and practice seemingly devoid of morality. So is the acquisition of knowledge of all kinds. As for sexual mores, anything goes. After all, does the state really care if its citizens are virtuous? It does so only to the extent that they obey the law and become productive members of the economy. But this wasn't always the case. Our state of economic affairs and the fracturing of our knowledge will be the subjects of the next chapter.

3.

Where We Are

The Economy and the Fracturing of Our Lives

Of the many facets of our fractured lives, I would argue that the divorcing of economics from morality bears the most practical consequences in our daily lives. Wrong political choices by those in power can certainly affect whether or or not we die in war, but most people's day-to-day lives do not seem to be directly affected by such choices, at least not in America. On the other hand, we spend forty to eighty hours a week working, depending on the professions we hold. When we take out the number of hours we spend sleeping and add commuting time to and from work, our jobs are where we spend the vast majority of our lives. Aside from work, a good portion of hours per week is also spent shopping, whether online or at a brick-and-mortar store. And I'm not just talking about America's mall addiction. Anyone with children knows that just grocery shopping can be a grueling trip that takes place several times a week. So for all practical purposes, we are producers and consumers at large. It seems that we are then more than what we eat, as the common refrain goes. Rather, we are what we produce and consume.

So how exactly did we come to think that such a gargantuan portion of our lives is devoid of morality? The rise of the secular nation-state, as explained in the previous chapter, meant that it also took on the role of provider, distributor, and regulator of economic goods. Because the state does not claim to take sides with any particular moral values, when it comes to the economy, so long as it is growing, the production and sale of almost anything is permissible and even encouraged. From electric cars to gas-guzzling Bentleys, from fair-trade coffee to sweat-shop-produced shoes, from gospel music to Marilyn Manson, just about anything goes as long as people want it. What have been the consequences of living in this political and economic arrangement?

THE TRIUMPH OF THE FREE MARKET

If we see the world from a purely materialistic point of view, it is important to first recognize that things have worked out quite well under the current system. Under the watch of the nation-state, the economy has delivered, and it has delivered well. The free market has pulled billions out of poverty, which seems in some ways to be a great and noble cause that the church should support. The American economy has worked miracles, so to speak. How did it do so? What are the origins of this material success?

After the dawn of nation-states, all countries have been somewhere within a spectrum between adopting a free market on one end and adopting a command economy on the other end. The last seventy years have sufficiently shown the triumph of the free market over command economies. The Soviet Union, once a global superpower, collapsed in 1991 purely for economic reasons, without a shot being fired. Pacifists could learn something here. In communist China, Mao's Great Leap Forward was shown to be really a Great Leap Backward as it led to the starvation of tens of millions. Once again this happened purely for economic reasons as Mao never intended this for anyone. Because it was lucidly evident that capitalism provided more abundant prosperity, China has now turned their economy in a more capitalist direction, though preserving a semblance of a politically communist state. Starting from the 1980s under the more free-market policies of Deng Xiaoping, China has steadily made economic progress. Now China is the second largest economy, threatening to dethrone America's place in the coming decades. In North Korea, perhaps the last bastion of communism, people have been starving for the last seventy years, while just across its southern border over 90 percent of South Koreans graduate from college. South Koreans have to thank a free market for their prosperous fate, which stands in stark contrast to their northern neighbors.

People on the left that love to deride capitalism and its excesses have to admit that the free market has lifted up billions of people out of poverty, not only now but from the moment of its inception. There is a reason why the Industrial Revolution started in Britain, which in turn became the empire so vast that the sun never set. The political freedoms that the state granted its citizens protected and encouraged private industry. The Industrial Revolution made it possible to mass-produce goods, making them more affordable, which in turn democratized the economy. Things that in the past were luxuries enjoyed only by aristocrats were now common among everyday folk.

This movement also had its own philosophical justification. In *The Wealth of Nations*, Adam Smith posited that when the state does not interfere in the economic activities of its own people, there is strangely an "invisible hand" guiding the economy towards prosperity. This is because when people are free to produce and buy what they want for the price that they want, their own personal incentives guide the economy collectively, which is more efficient than a bureaucratic system trying to do so. People's desire to have their economic needs and wants met is a sufficient incentive for them to produce or work for what consumers are willing to pay them. Competition then prods them to produce those goods with higher quality at a lower cost. In short, the free market works so well because it produces the goods that people want. How could the state or some other bureaucratic institution even fathom the enormous task of guessing what the people need and want? That would be foolish and inefficient. If I'm a farmer and my costumers start demanding strawberries rather than mangoes, I'll make sure I bring them strawberries next time around to earn their business and everyone will be happy, producer and consumer alike. I do not need the government or other institutions, but rather my customers, to tell me what to produce. If a business fails, it is only because it failed to produce what people were looking for at the right price.

The workings of a free market should be so obvious there might be readers that wonder why I bother explaining it. As it turns out, after capitalism has succeeded for the last seventy years, bashing capitalism seems to be a fad on the rise once again among liberals. There are many things that they get right in their criticisms, as we'll see, but it's tempting to throw the baby out with the bathwater in the polarized times that we live in. If lifting people out of poverty is a cause worth pursuing by the church, we should not forget why and how the free market works. In many respects, the current economic system is in part the legacy of the church's past, as I will show later. Even if there are problems with the free market, I do not think that socialism enforced by the state is the answer, as history has lucidly shown. As a matter of fact, there are some aspects of the current system that the church can and should embrace.

It's not just its triumph against communism that validates the free market as an effective system. In recent years, the United Nations released their Millennium Development Goals report. The UN has a number of goals it wants to achieve for the general betterment of humanity, such as eradicating extreme poverty and hunger, achieving universal primary education, reducing child mortality, etc. The UN also had specific improvement benchmarks for each goal. As it turns out, the 2015 report shows that some of these goals were not only achieved, but were surpassed. It so happens that the region leading the progress by far was Eastern Asia. For instance, one of the targets was to halve the proportion of people whose income is less than one dollar a day from 1990 to 2015. As it turns out, it was not only halved, but the proportion went down a whopping 94 percent in China.[60] Another target was to reduce by two thirds the under-five mortality rate. As it turn out, it went down 78 percent in Eastern Asia.[61] To what can we attribute this success? It should be clearly evident that the economic liberalization that took place under Deng Xiaoping started to bear fruit back in the 1990s. Because China is the most populous country in the world, the salubrious consequences of the free market were magnified. Isn't it remarkable that the simple introduction of liberal economic policies to what was once a very poor country achieved more than any program or humanitarian aid of NGOs or religious organizations, churches included? And here, once again, the state was the savior, not the church. When the world is better at achieving a goal that the church sees eye to eye with, I think it calls for self-reflection on the part of the church: why did we fail while others got it right? Of course, the church cannot always follow the sometimes violent means of the world, but the question is still worth asking time to time.

THE FAILURES OF THE FREE MARKET

But what then shall we say about the free-market system? Is it so wonderful that it merits our applause? Should church leaders simply acquiesce to the godless market and encourage their congregants to keep shopping and prop up the state? There are many Christians who have. I don't need to mention by name organizations that explicitly do so. One only needs to hear what prosperity preachers are saying. But if we honestly examine the narrative of our lives individually and communally, we would discover that even if we find ourselves well-off financially, this system still leaves much to be desired (quite literally).

The 2008 financial crisis showed clearly how fragile the whole system is. After over eight million people lost their jobs, the average household lost about a quarter of its net worth, and over a hundred banks failed,[62] the state was forced to actively intervene to save the system. The government bailed out all the major banks, saved the car industry, printed trillions of dollars, and bought out bad mortgages. So much for the invisible hand. Can any free-market advocate really say that the government should have done nothing while people were losing their jobs and their homes? 2008 proved that there can be no such thing as a fully invisible hand. Results cannot be good when we are all left to our own greed, individually and collectively.

Though it has improved the overall standard of living of billions, the free market has also widened the gap between the wealthy and the poor. In 1980, the bottom 50 percent of the U.S. population took in about $16,000 of income whereas the top 1 percent took in about $400,000. Adjusted for inflation, in 2014, the top 1 percent took in about $1,300,000 while the bottom 50% still took in about $16,000.[63] Why does the free market lead to a widening gap? There are many factors of course, but to put it simply, money makes money. Those who have better incomes are able to invest their disposable income to generate even more income. Anyone who is a landlord can testify how much easier it is to generate money when you start off with some. That means that those who have better incomes are able to multiply their returns exponentially and then pass on their wealth to their children. Is this just the result of the market rewarding prudence and merit? Maybe to an extent. But here it simply will not do to justify the free market by saying that all that matters is that most people were lifted up economically. The problem of a widening gap is that it creates a vast gulf between social classes to the extent that those on the lower rungs become so completely other. Does it really matter that poor people can now afford iPhones or 4K TVs, given that they have been "lifted up" by the general market? The reality is that those items do not gain them any respect in society as they become part of an inescapable lower social rung. So much for community.

The soulless character of the economy is also in full display when a company decides to move its jobs overseas just to pursue higher profit margins. Americans have lost millions upon millions of jobs over the last few decades due to outsourcing. Being fed up of it altogether, many cast their votes with Trump. But really, per the goals and rules of the free market, if the market is "rational" to any extent, then the purpose of a company is to make profits. So why not dispose of your workers in pursuit of cheaper labor? What else did we expect when we embraced this system? And so companies and their goods move across borders while people cannot always do so. As a result, many of the products we consume are produced in factories where workers often get paid cents per hour and work under horrid conditions. Of course, one can always justify this saying that those workers are better off with a bad job than without one. Maybe. But if we as buyers met the workers directly one on one, would we really pay them what they get paid? When one considers the moral ambiguities of our current system, it becomes clear that one is a sinner just by virtue of being part of the global economy. All the while, we produce hundreds of millions of tons of garbage a year because we are a throwaway society. In the wall of my classroom I have a poster inspired by *The Fight Club* that reads, "We buy things we don't need, with money we don't have, to impress people we don't like." Some of us justify our consumerism by thinking it provides jobs, that it keeps the economy moving. As for the environment, we'll let our grandchildren deal with it. Given that little of that mountain of trash gets recycled, God knows where it all ends up.

I'd like to think that we are all aware of these problems, whether we are conservative or liberal. I understand that there are some who refuse to believe some of the specifics, such as human-induced climate change. But can anyone really deny that we are polluting the Earth overall? Then why do so many embrace the current system? I refuse to believe that it's just that people are generally so callous, but rather I think it's that they see no better alternative. Communism was a horrible experiment, so there is no way we are going to embrace that. So we are content to live in a quasi-free market protected by the state, which on occasion swings a little bit to the left, then a little bit to the right, depending on who is in control.

THE ECONOMY AND MORAL FORMATION

Yet I think the church cannot afford to ignore other problems of our current arrangement. What if the market not only affects others on some remote village, or the environment for that matter? What if it affects our very own moral formation? Because the economy is provided to us by a non-religious and supposedly morally neutral nation-state, it has led us into the fracturing of our lives in which we assume that the economy is completely devoid from morality or faith. We tend to think that finances are a personal matter. But if we examine our current arrangement carefully and what it does to us, we would find that this is not the case at all.

First, let's talk about moral formation from the consumer's side. Cavanaugh points out that the problem with consumerism is that it makes people misplace their desires onto just stuff. How can we call this a "free market" when in reality we have just become slaves of our possessions or our way of life? Quoting Augustine's famous words "our hearts are restless until they rest in you," Cavanaugh states that God should be the true object of our desires.[64] Yet the market ends up shaping our desires more than the church. Given that we spend several hours a week on television and the Internet, but only an hour at church, we are then bombarded with advertisements telling us to desire stuff we don't really need.[65]

I would go even further and argue that the matter is even worse when we look at moral formation from the producer's side. Like I've said, we spend the vast majority of our lives at our workplace. How did we imagine that it would have no moral bearing on us? Perhaps we have been trained to think that business is just business, not personal.

Here I think it is important to first clarify that a very important part of moral formation is the formation of virtues and vices. This is a bit different from modernity's conception of ethics. The Enlightenment trained our society to think that ethics is all about making the most rational choices at the right time. So, for instance, what would be the right thing to do in the following scenario, which was vividly portrayed at a Harvard lecture? Assume that a trolley car has lost its brakes and is about to crash into five workers. You are an onlooker standing on a bridge over the tracks. Next to you there is a very obese man leaning over. You could give him a little push so he falls on the tracks and stops the trolley or you could let the five workers die.[66] As rational as they are, Enlightenment philosophers cannot come to an agreement as to what is the right choice here. Utilitarians would tell you to push over the obese man, to put it crudely, whereas Immanuel Kant would say that you should just watch the five workers die.

But virtue ethics is a bit different from this kind of situational ethics. Virtues and vices make up our character and are built up over time by habit, not just thorough one situation. So one is habituated to do what is right by continuously training oneself to choose the good in the small things on a regular basis. Then when a weightier situation arises, the person will naturally choose to do what is right, without blinking, because it had been her habit to do so. It's not so much like she has a choice, for she is bound by her habit to either do the good or the bad.

It is important to note that the church had always believed in the virtues up until the time of the Enlightenment. Character is built up by constant practice of the good, making what Jesus said true: "Whoever is faithful in a very little is faithful also in much" (Luke 16:10). Many Christians believe that one should become thoroughly a better person at the moment that one is saved or comes to know the Lord. And yes, fundamentally, there is a world of difference when one becomes a Christian, as one becomes a new creation with a completely new perspective on things. But that doesn't mean that one is suddenly so perfect as to not need to strive for the virtues. Why else would Paul say, "I want to know Christ and the power of the resurrection and the sharing of his sufferings by becoming like him in his death" (Phil 3:10)?[67] Didn't he already know Christ after meeting him on his way to Damascus? Paul could have only said so because the virtues require constant practice towards a goal.

Different cultures have come up with their own list of virtues based on what they have deemed of primary importance. But for the church, Paul said, "the fruit of the Spirit is love, joy, peace, patience, kindness, generosity, faithfulness, gentleness, and self-control" (Gal 5:22).[68] Many Christians think that when one receives the Spirit, one suddenly becomes more loving, joyous, and gentle. After all, a lot of items in this list seem like emotional qualities on the surface. But if that is the case, what can be said of patience and self-control? Surely, those are virtues that are built up over time by constant practice with the guidance of the Spirit. Later on the church came up with the seven virtues of prudence, justice, temperance, courage, faith, hope, and love, which are not that different from the Pauline list above.

If indeed the virtues (or vices) require practice on a regular basis, where do we suppose most of that practice takes place—at church or at the workplace? This is precisely the problem of the church having withdrawn to the role of therapist for a couple hours a week. The reality is that most of our virtues and vices are built up where we spend the most time, at the corporation, the government, or school if we happen to be students. So ultimately the economy is not really neutral when it comes to morality. Every corporation, every school, every government has its own culture, and with that its own implicit list of virtues and vices. It's as though every corporation is a religion on its own terms.

Consider that one of the earliest definitions of virtue is that of excellence in whatever one does. In his *Ethics,* Aristotle says, "The virtues . . . we acquire by first having put them into action, and the same is also true of the arts. For the things which we have to learn before we can do them we learn by doing: men become builders by building houses, and harpists by playing the harp."[69] The analogy is clearly made to almost any economic activity one can think of, which goes to show that the ancients never for a moment divorced economics from morality.

What then are the virtues or vices being subliminally fed to us by our corporations? Obviously each company has its own set of values, some of them worse than others. If one worked for Stratton Oakmont, the fund managed by the "Wolf of Wall Street," one probably would find oneself continuously practicing the vices of pride, lust, gluttony, and greed. Of course, most workplaces are not that depraved. Most companies are just trying to make a buck. Thus most people learn the discipline of hard work, self-denial, and prudence in most workplaces. As for integrity and courage, it's a hit or miss. Some companies value them, some don't. But regardless, the corporation has become a much more relevant place than church in cultivating the virtues.

If the virtues require constant practice, another closely related concept is discipline by correction. We build habits through correction or lack thereof. If the church is composed of a people called to holiness, then there has to be discipline in the church. Obviously the church should not use physical force to discipline its members. Instead, Jesus taught us that discipline should take place as prescribed in Matthew 18, where it says that if a person sins, he or she should first be told directly in private. If he does not listen, then he should be confronted with two or three witnesses. If he or she still does not listen, then the church should be told. And finally if she still persists, then she should be treated as a Gentile or tax collector, who at that time were considered outsiders of the Jewish community. In other words, the final recourse that any church has is to excommunicate or kick out someone from its community. Some churches practice this by not allowing those members to take part of Communion.

But given that many churches today are competing for dwindling numbers, they are not inclined to discipline their members. And how can they, given that there isn't much at stake in the church anyways? If people do not feel in need of therapy or socializing, why would they care if the church disciplines them? They can just leave to the church next block. On the other hand, there is a lot at stake when one works for a company or is enrolled in a school. "Excommunication" from such places would mean getting fired or expelled, which would result in the loss of a salary or a degree. So ultimately it is the corporation or a school that holds all the cards. They, not the church, are the ones who get to discipline their members and thus form the virtues or vices.

THE ECONOMY AND MEANING

But it's not just for the virtues or vices that the workplace or school has surpassed the church in relevance. Ultimately, the endeavor where most of our time is consumed gets to shape the meaning of our lives. That means that for a lot of people the corporations they work for get to shape much of the purpose of their existence. As mirror images of their host state, most corporations are devoid of moral values or a purpose other than making a quick buck, which in turn makes many a job a miserable grind devoid of any meaning. No wonder why so many hate their jobs, yet continue making the trek every morning simply because they need the money. All the while, they cannot see how anything they do at work has any connection to their religious beliefs.

We millennials are a much-derided generation, often with good reason I admit. We can't manage to stay in one job for thirty or forty years as our parents used to do, apparently because we are entitled, lazy tech junkies lacking any sense of commitment to any social body. An employer would be lucky if she managed to keep one of us for five years. Though much of the opprobrium is well deserved, our seeming lack of commitment is sometimes for good reason. As it turns out, millennials are people who want to work with a sense of purpose for a good cause.[70] If we can't find it in a given company, we'll move to another one. We also want a sense of community in the workplace, as we would prefer to work in collaborative teams than in cubicles.[71]

Given that this is the case, not everyone hates their job. Once millennials find the right place, they end up loving their work. There are a number of companies loved by millennials whose mission transcends profits. For instance, part of Tesla's mission statement is to "accelerate the world's transition to sustainable energy."[72] Thanks to founder Elon Musk's persistent vision, Tesla is at the forefront of the renewable energy industry. It is remarkable that a private company is bound to have more positive impact on the environment than our stripped-down version of the EPA. Another one of Musk's companies, SpaceX, has the goal of "enabling people to live on other planets."[73] This gets its workers so fired up that every time there is a successful rocket launch the company headquarters is beaming with excitement. Good for them, but one has to wonder, why is a place like SpaceX more exciting than church? Why does a non-religious company like Tesla get to do more for the environment than the church? Is it any wonder that millennials have found the church to be increasingly irrelevant? There was a time when the church was at the forefront of scientific research and technological innovation, as I will show later, but not anymore.

Recent attempts have been made to relate our daily jobs, whether exciting or not, to the life of faith. Influenced by Luther and Calvin, Lee Hardy and Timothy Keller point out that we need to recover a sense of vocation, which is more than simply the work we do from nine to five. The common good and social responsibility are no doubt part of that vocation.[74] Keller furthers the argument by making us see ourselves as part of a larger narrative, the gospel story, which then affects the way we envision work. According to the gospel, the world was made good, it is now fallen, yet it will be redeemed.[75] This narrative will no doubt shape how one decides to practice business, medicine, journalism, education, and the arts. For instance, when it comes to journalism, one does not simply report from a purely objective standpoint. One has to write a story with heroes and villains in it, which no doubt will be shaped from the author's worldview.[76] A Christian manager would be prone to balancing the interests of shareholders, customers, employees, suppliers, and the surrounding community, rather than simply pursuing profits.[77] In the same vein, the Catholic position is that work is a dimension of our being created in the image of God to subdue the Earth.[78] Work then should reflect that divine creative process in its dignity towards oneself, others, and creation. The way all of this often translates into practical advice is that one is in a way baptizing one's work by bringing the Christian worldview into it. Work ultimately contributes to the flourishing and advancement of humanity, which is our task as creatures created in God's image. This is God's plan that God intended for human work, so the argument goes.

Though much of this is true, I would argue that furthering these noble goals alone should not make a Christian content with her work accomplishments. In *The City of God*, Augustine contrasts the city of man versus the city of God. He observes that, in contrast to Seth's line, the first city of man, the one that Cain built, was corrupt. It was "a city in which nothing more is hoped for than can be seen in this world."[79] One can clearly see though that the city that Cain built was flourishing in every conceivable way. First of all, they raised livestock, which was often preceded by the development of agriculture in order to feed oneself and one's animals. Then the text says that they forged iron, which in ancient times was an advanced metal, stronger than bronze. This represents the advancement of technology in this city. They also played the lyre and the pipe, which means that the city was thriving in the arts and culture (Gen 4:20–22). Only an abundance of basic resources could have afforded some of the spare time needed for such leisurely activities. In other words, the city of Cain is depicted as a thriving and bustling city that negated God's punishment on Cain to be fruitless and a wanderer. Yet that same place is depicted as a depraved city. It was the home of Lamech, the first person in the Bible to have two wives and who boasted of killing someone (Gen 4:23–24). On the other hand, the descendants of Seth become those who "invoke the name of the Lord" (Gen 4:26) thereby continuing the city of God. No major technological or cultural achievements are mentioned about them.

The same critique of godless human advancement can be said of the Tower of Babel story a few chapters later. In that story, humans are united and settle in one place in order to build a tower that reaches to the heavens, making a name for themselves. They had brick for stone and bitumen for mortar, showing their technological prowess. When God looks at what they are doing he observes that nothing will be impossible for them (Gen 11:1–7).

What these stories go to show is that merely pursuing the flourishing or beautification of human civilization simply does not cut it as a vocation for Christians. Though a noble goal, this alone cannot infuse our daily jobs with enough significance. This may not sit well for many who work corporate jobs. Many church leaders have taken the therapeutic route, making people feel better about their jobs by either saying that it is a vocation given by God where they must do their best, that their job contributes to the flourishing and advancement of humankind, or by showing them that their work is another outlet where they can spread the gospel. There is certainly a lot of truth in all of these statements. But the goal of this book is not to provide therapy. If our job sucks, then it sucks! No amount of tricking our brain to think that we are making a positive contribution will do. If we work merely for a greedy money-making machine, then our life is a part of that. The goal that Christians should have in any endeavor should not be simply to contribute to the betterment of humanity, which often gets intertwined with nation building. Rather, the true goal of Christians should be to serve and build up the church. Anything else, though grand or noble, is at the end of the day just another Babel tower.

Germany's case is worth mentioning once again. Germany was and is a great nation that has produced industry, culture, and great thinkers. But the German church, erroneously thinking that its goal was to preserve such greatness, threw its support behind someone who committed the worst crimes in human history. There is no doubt that America too is a great nation, at the cutting edge of most innovation in almost every field. But the American church must not make the same mistake in thinking that its goal is the preservation of this great culture, thereby encouraging Christians to work for the flourishing of the nation and humanity. If we are Christians, this isn't our true home after all.

THE ECONOMY AND COMMUNITY

Loneliness is a rampant problem afflicting the West. Many flock to the church yearning for a sense of community, and though some do find a sense of brotherhood or sisterhood in it, many others fail to find community there. On the other hand, there are many who find community in their school and in their workplace. Why might that be? This is not just a matter of the hours spent per week on each institution, though obviously that plays a major role. What contributes significantly to a group of people bonding together is a common sense of purpose and an economic commitment to each other. When the church becomes merely a social club or therapist, it fails to provide these two necessities. One might think that being a social club full of nice people would yield a better sense of community. But without a clear unified purpose, such community is shallow at best. On the other hand, a corporation has a common purpose to which all its members are expected to contribute.

As an analogy, let us consider the family, the social unit that is generally the most cohesive of all. Family members are the closest people one can have, not always because they are the most fun to hang out with. I'm sure many can remember many a family dinner fight. But a family is essentially an economic unit. Family members are the closest because, generally, family members take care of each other, not just emotionally, but also economically. I understand that not all families do so, and there are some couples who even sign a prenuptial so that they do not fully share their possessions.

That this is the case only goes to show how even the concept of family has become corrupted by individualistic influences.

Yet God intended couples to have a common purpose for which they would work and help each other, thereby cementing their bond. God said of the first couple, "It is not good for the man to be alone. I will make a helper suitable for him" (Gen 2:18). When thinking about the purpose of marriage, many take the first part seriously. They correctly believe that the purpose of marriage is to have a lifelong companion that will help them avoid loneliness. But many ignore the second part of the verse, which is to help each other out. The verse begs the question, help to do what? Many have thought that this speaks to the fact that life is full of hardships and people generally need to help each other. That is true, but one must keep in mind that this verse is part of Genesis 2, a description of paradise, before hardships as we know them came into the world. As it turns out, a surprising part of this paradise is also that God gives humanity *work* to be done. It is said a couple of verses earlier, "God took the man and put him in the garden of Eden to work it and keep it" (Gen 2:15). Many picture paradise to be a leisurely place of rest with not much to do. But that is not the description of biblical paradise. Work provides meaning and purpose to our lives and hence it is a necessity for our souls. So man and woman were bound to each other, being given a common sense of purpose to do God's good work. That many marriages end up in divorce today speaks to the lack of purpose to which many come together, except to have fun with each other.

Going back to society as a whole, part of the problem is that in today's society one is more prone to find a more meaningful purpose at work or at school, and therefore find more meaningful friendships there than at church. The corporation has become the true meritocracy in which one is valued and respected for the skills that one contributes to the corporation. It is in corporate America that those that are quiet introverts can truly shine based on the merit of their work contribution. I believe that introverts, of which I count myself as one, are in some ways a forgotten minority. Much has been said about how other minority groups have faced neglect, such as African Americans, immigrants, women, etc., but not much about introverts. Because we introverts are generally quiet and unassertive, our opinions often get ignored in many a social occasion or meeting, whether in college or at church. We could never possibly be the life of the party and are often overlooked as uninteresting people. But once at work, our value is not always tied to how much we talk, but to the quality of our work. There are many, including myself, whom I have seen at a workplace suddenly gain respect and friendships who would usually not have stood a chance in a party-like setting. I am sure many an introvert can relate to this (though they would very likely not openly express it). This is how powerful work can be in providing community.

Speaking of minorities, in any party-like setting people by nature tend to congregate among those who are most like them. After all, the saying that birds of a feather flock together is true, given that people usually feel most comfortable among people like themselves. But what this comes to mean is that minorities often end up neglected in such party-like environments. Yet when it comes down to business, one cannot afford to ignore the economic contribution that every sizable group makes, either as producer or consumer. Is it any surprise that businesses interact across racial and ethnic lines significantly more than the church? Martin Luther King Jr. once said that Sunday at 11 o'clock is the most segregated hour in America. But what else can one expect if church has become merely a party where people tend to flock with those who are most like themselves? To our shame, businesses do a much better job at integration than the church. This happens both on the consumer and producer side. On the consumer side, businesses cannot afford to discriminate based on race or religion, for that would decrease a significant portion of their market. And on the producer side, businesses need reliable workers to accomplish their goals regardless of their skin color or gender.

Moreover, one often cannot afford to stop business merely for small grudges. In a workplace, people have to put their small differences aside in order to accomplish a common goal, and in doing so some end up tolerating their differences. The same goes for businesses dealing with consumers. Businesses often cannot afford to hold grudges against consumers. They have to keep "forgiving" them, so to speak, in order to win their loyalty. In this respect, it is a shame that just about any godless corporation, such as Goldman Sachs or Apple, has become a more redeeming place than the church.

One may object here that having "shop talk" with someone about work is not being in community. But I suspect that to many of us (introverts especially) shop talk is a lot more meaningful and interesting than small talk, which often is the talk after a Sunday service. If someone finds shop talk—let's say talk about computer science—too geeky and uninteresting, it is only because of the failure of our churches to apply that knowledge in meaningful ways. As such, most of our shop talk ends up being about our contribution to a godless and greedy corporation, which for outsiders is simply too geeky and boring. But if such talk were properly integrated into advancing the causes of the church, it certainly would be more interesting than small talk. For many, small talk after the Sunday service often ends up becoming about someone's last vacation, the latest movie, or the last football game someone watched. It's not the most interesting of conversations, to say the least, which fails to truly bind people together in meaningful ways.

If work then is a necessity for our souls that binds us to one another, what exactly is the work that the church provides today? Some churches are of course more missional than others. Some encourage their members to spread the gospel in some way or another, though it is not always clear how members are to do so. The reality is that there aren't many venues of work in the church that would genuinely consume one's time, energy, and passion as it should. For a lot of churches, the only meaningful roles one can hold are that of pastor and worship leader. But what can one do if one is not a good preacher or a musician? Shouldn't there be other jobs to serve God with? How exactly is one supposed to practice Paul's famous dictum that we all have our different gifts to contribute to the church (1 Cor 12:12–31)? So many Christians end up sitting passively on the back pews. That's a shame given that worship in the early church was participatory. But the work of the church is supposed to be so compelling and exciting that it draws all members into it. It should be the salvific work that the church, and only the whole church, can do.

Many here would object that a meritocracy is not exactly a system that Christians should embrace. Shouldn't Christians value all people, regardless of merit or skill? Besides, aren't business relationships transactional and therefore conditional? Shouldn't our relationships reflect God's one-sided unconditional love towards us? There is certainly a lot of truth in all of these objections. I would argue, however, that the position from which these questions arise neglects some key aspects of the nature of human relationships. Although it is true that God's love is unconditional, this does not mean that God has no expectations from us whatsoever. God's unconditional love speaks to God loving us as we are, but God in God's love still has expectations from us. Scripture makes it clear that there are many precepts that we are expected to obey. God may still love us whether or not we follow God, but God still expects us to follow God. A parent would treat a child in similar fashion. Moreover, we were meant to be givers as well as receivers. Relationships are meant to be reciprocal. We were created to naturally feel delight about giving or contributing something for someone. That's why, in exploring friendship, Aristotle says that friendships "are based on equality; both partners receive and wish the same thing from and for one another."[80] One would not feel complete whether one is solely the giver or the receiver in a relationship. As a matter of fact, it would be more offensive if a recipient did not appreciate the gifts given to him than if someone received no gifts at all. That is why one feels affirmation at being recognized for a contribution at work.

Still, one may object that this excludes people who are unable to contribute to the workforce. What of those with disabilities, one may ask? Here I would answer that this way of thinking is the result of our perceptions being distorted by what the world has to say about such people. The vast majority of so-called disabled persons are still capable of contributing something of value, and would actually very much want to do so. To deny them work because they seem incapable of much would be the biggest insult to them. In *Resident Aliens*, Hauerwas and Willimon offer a concrete example of a woman by the name of Dorothy in a church's third-grade class. She was in charge of handing out pencils and checking the names of children in the roll book. The authors describe that "it was much later, when we were nearly all grown up and adult, that the world told us that she was someone with Down Syndrome. At the church, we were under the impression that she was the teacher's assistant."[81] The identity and value that a polity gives a person can be a world of difference depending on the type of politics it is. When Dorothy died, the whole church turned out for her funeral. Fortunately for Dorothy, her church was an alternative politics that embraced her gifts and she was therefore given meaningful work to do. But not all persons like her would be so lucky. It is sad that some private companies would be able to provide more meaningful work for people like Dorothy than many churches, when churches are supposed to be the places of genuine communion with one another. Like I said, regardless of whether or not they are disabled, most people simply do not have the gift of preaching or singing. On the other hand, corporations have a need to take on a wide diversity of gifts that people have to offer, even those of the disabled.

Is it therefore any surprise that people, particularly millennials, are finding a more inclusive community outside of the church? Is it any surprise that people are finding more meaning and excitement in corporations, or more discipline and the cultivation of virtues in academic institutions? No wonder why people are leaving the church in droves.

THE FRACTURING OF KNOWLEDGE

In Western societies, before one enters the workforce, a significant portion of one's time is spent in school. From the moment one enters preschool all the way to college, kids and young adults spend a good thirty-five hours a week in school, not counting the time spent on homework and other after-school activities. Those that pursue an advanced degree often continue in academia all the way into their thirties. This means once again that for much of the early portion of our lives, moral formation, purpose, and community are to be found in school, more so than in the church. Because the vast majority of kids end up attending a public school sponsored by a non-religious state, education becomes devoid of any religious values. If the public schools teach any values at all, they are either limited to so-called civic virtues that encourage good citizenship or aim for the so-called self-actualization of each child as an individual. So, for instance, students are to recite the Pledge of Allegiance every morning facing the flag. They are taught to recycle, to respect public officers, to not bully, to not do drugs, to to use protection when having sex, and so on. They are also taught their nation's history, how their government works, and how to civically engage in a democracy.

As for self-actualization, education schools where teachers get their training endorse methods derived from child psychology. So the aim often becomes to raise children that have self-esteem, are compassionate, show leadership, and have critical thinking skills. In the process, methods such as lecturing to students are derided as monotonous techniques that do not sufficiently make students think for themselves. So children end up either being raised as good citizens for their nation or being given inflated egos that make them incapable of being followers for once.

And here, once again, how much can Sunday school raise kids as Christians, given that it takes place only for an hour a week whereas one attends school for a good thirty-five hours a week? Moreover, resources for discipline are limited in a church given that students are not really given a grade, whereas there is a lot at stake in school. All of this doesn't even take into account that many kids are being raised by the values implicit in TV and the Internet more so than the values that their busy parents often fail to provide. Besides, many of the parents themselves have already bought in to the values offered by TV and the Internet.

Upon high school graduation some make it to college. Of course, the higher education landscape ends up becoming somewhat more diverse than what kids had for high school choices. There are public or private, religious or non-religious, academically minded or party-centered schools to choose from. Yet the way universities are structured is similar across the board. There are numerous fields of study with their various departments. Each professor in each department is basically under a "publish or perish" contract before tenureship. This means that the system encourages specialization to the extent that professors' research interests often focus on minutiae not relevant to the real world. Why would the average person benefit from such knowledge? Besides, because only novel ideas get published, this means that professors will usually be subversive of the status quo and will in turn teach students to do so. This isn't always bad, but not all traditions have to be done away with. The focus on novel research is part of the reason why colleges usually have a liberal bias. Moreover, the fact that professors are paid to do research means that many of them are just plain incompetent teachers. I once had a professor whose lecture consisted of only reading the textbook he had published in front of the class, barely making eye contact. The worst part about all of this is that after a student has incurred a debt of tens of thousands of dollars, if not hundreds of thousands, they often do not know how to integrate much of the knowledge they acquired. What exactly is the relationship between nuclear fission and Hesiod's works? Does one's faith have any connection to it at all?

This fragmentation of various fields of knowledge is not without consequence. Because many fail to integrate the natural sciences with the humanities, they often have the misperception that only the sciences offer the purest, most concrete objective truths. Though many of us claim to be religious, most of us live as materialists in practice—believing that the sciences and their resulting technologies provide the best solutions to human problems. Technology's ability to solve many of our problems is certainly without dispute, but an uncritical optimism of everything technological is also problematic.

Philosophers of science and epistemology have demonstrated that even the sciences are deserving of a bit of healthy skepticism. One such skeptic, David Hume, went as far as questioning the very concept of cause and effect, which is at the core of how science operates. Our knowledge is constrained by the limits of our brain's ability to perceive the world around us. The reality is that our brains are not wired to be objective by simply taking in raw facts, but they are wired to interpret the facts and give them meaning, which in turn may lead to biases. According to Hume, what we call "cause and effect" is an instance of our brains interpreting facts, not the raw facts themselves. Suppose that a billiard ball hits another and makes it move. We tend to think that the first ball caused the effect of the second ball moving. But really, the raw fact of what we are seeing is merely that the movement of the first ball preceded that of the second.[82] Hume also points out that our sight is only able to perceive a series of colored dots, nothing more.[83] Think of our sight as a series of pixels on a screen. What we perceive as movement is merely the pixels changing colors. So even the idea of movement is put into question by Hume.

If one thinks that Hume goes too far, one should consider the problem of induction. Scientific axioms are merely conjectures that rest simply on that our experience has shown them to work so far. But does that mean it rests on logic? We know that, logically, just because something has worked in the past, it is not guaranteed to work in the future. Just because the stock market has been on a tear for the last ten years, it is not guaranteed to continue going up indefinitely. In the same vein, just because a lab experiment produced a certain result, there is no logical guarantee that it should repeat itself. So it is the case that Newtonian physics used to work for a while, until it was shown that it just didn't do its job when measuring large or very fast things. But if Einstein's general relativity seems to have replaced Newtonian physics, the reality is that Einstein's theory just doesn't work for very small particles. Currently, the discrepancies between quantum physics and general relativity are puzzling to say the least.

So why exactly do many believe that science is all there is to knowledge? Why do some despise religious beliefs as unproven conjectures when many scientific axioms also require faith in their own sense? There has to be some level of respect and awe for the transcendent when one looks at the beauty and wonder of the universe. Even though not a Christian, Einstein at least had some respect for the transcendent, whereas many scientists who do not come close to him in brilliance have an air of arrogance in them. But such has been the effect of the fracturing of the different fields of knowledge.

Close examination of the politics of scientific research should also restrain our unquestioned credence for the sciences. Ultimately, who gets to fund the production of knowledge matters in the way data comes out and how it is used. We tend to think that research, especially the scientific kind, should be objective. But postmodernism has shown that complete objectivity is impossible to achieve. After all, research will always be guided by the motivations of those who partake of and pay for it. And can motivations be morally neutral? The state will always fund or encourage research ultimately for its own aggrandizement. The state fully understands that any particular advancement that takes place under its territory is ultimately beneficial to itself, and therefore funds it directly or encourages it through policy. After all, a strong economy is considered a matter of national security, for only a robust economy can support a powerful army. But sometimes it is more direct than that. Numerous technological advancements can be used for warfare, even if originally not intended for that. Consider, for instance, the Google employee protests against their company's innovations being appropriated by the Department of Defense.[84]

But corporations and even universities are not significantly different from the state. The purpose of the research they fund may not necessarily be to create an army, but it is done ultimately for the corporation's or university's own aggrandizement, which in turn is always influenced by economics. For instance, what could possibly be the motivation behind candy and soft drink makers researching the effects of sugar intake? Could such research be conducted without bias? Not surprisingly, the result of the research was that recommendations on limiting sugar intake were based on weak evidence.[85] But this is not limited to corporations' direct research. That would make it easy to differentiate that data as compromised. Now numerous university professors are participating in this privately funded research and have signed non-disclosure agreements, making it difficult to distinguish biased from less biased research.[86] Who pays the bills matters at the end. It tells us very clearly who people work for. As more universities are strapped for cash, they will find and even encourage other sources of funding. But can even a university that takes no outside funding really claim that its research is produced completely free from bias? The reality is that all research will have its own bias based on the motivations of the researchers. For instance, is it surprising that an atheist scientist like Richard Dawkins will often display the cruelty of nature rather than its beauty? What else could possibly be his motivation other than to make his point that a good God does not exist?

Those who are not very academic minded may not be too perturbed about the current state of affairs. But part of the reason why I placed this section under the economics chapter is that knowledge eventually percolates into the economy. Sometimes it has a direct effect upon it. This is most evident in the way that the developments in the natural sciences directly affect industry innovation, whether on healthcare, energy, transportation, etc. If the place where knowledge originates is unable to relate its various branches with faith, let alone with one another, this will be naturally projected on the industries that acquire and implement that knowledge. Is it therefore any surprise that many corporations behave as though ethics have no bearings on them? Or even that they pursue innovations without fully considering ethical quandaries raised by them?

Consider the case of a couple doctors experimenting with head transplants in mice.[87] I will let the reader surmise on the sinister motivations behind such experiments. Even if one could claim that in the future a quadriplegic person may be able to receive another fully functional body, where exactly will this body come from? Has anyone thought about the ethics of such experimentation? Or how many technology companies and their CEOs are concerned about the ethical implications of the further advances that artificial intelligence will bring? Fortunately a few have spoken up regarding the potential dangers, such as Elon Musk and Bill Gates. Musk has called AI the greatest existential threat to humanity, not only because it will soon displace a significant portion of the workforce, but because he believes that at some point AI will become conscious, which could unleash havoc if it is already smarter than humans in many ways.[88] Yet because he is not a Christian, his solution has been to create Neuralink, a company devoted to producing internal brain meshes that will enable humans to directly communicate with machines.[89] Musk's solution is essentially that if we can't beat machines at their game, we'll have to become partially machines ourselves. Though Musk should be commended for sounding the alarm on unrestrained AI advancement, once again, where are the ethics in his solution? All the while, the rest of Silicon Valley luminaries as well as professors in the field seem to pursue AI's rapid advancement with unfettered optimism.

I'm not saying that science and technology are terrible endeavors that should be abolished. They should be advanced, but who conducts the research matters. It's a shame then that the church has dropped the ball on scientific research. If there will always be some level of bias, it would be best that a fully ethical politics like the church be responsible in the production of knowledge. But alas, the church today is mostly preoccupied with fixing people's personal relationships. How many theological ethics professors specialize in the quandaries of AI's advancement? How many seminaries pursue research on the field? I don't know of any. One could argue that this is naturally the case given that AI is a particularly difficult subject that requires technical expertise. So then, does that make us Christians a dim-witted bunch? Perhaps some of us are. Yet I have personally met some brilliant Christians pursuing doctorates in the field of machine learning. Once again, the problem here stems from the loss of interdisciplinary integration of various specialized fields so that those who pursue one field lack even cursory expertise or interest on another. In a few years from now, AI will arrive full force and the church will find itself ill prepared to provide any answers to its quandaries. Then the church will once again play catch-up, doing too little too late, just like it has on many other issues.

But this was not always the state of affairs. As I will show in the next chapter, the church was at the forefront of education during the Middle Ages. Monasteries initially led the way by having monks study the Scriptures. Because of their regimented work schedule, they also ended up studying subjects other than the Scriptures. Eventually, the medieval universities were formed in which theology was the queen of the sciences. Sadly, the specialization and fragmentation of knowledge was the natural result of having taken a Christian worldview out of knowledge, which was the inevitable result of the church retreating from the economy and the academy.

4.

Where We Came From

Theological Foundations

I have so far laid out numerous problems that are plaguing our society and the church. I said that the rise of the nation-state led to a diminished church as the state took over the numerous political and economic roles that the church had. This in turn led not only to a church that has lost relevance, but also to the fracturing of the many aspects of our lives while a secular and purportedly morally neutral state came to govern these various facets of life. It's easy to take for granted the current state of affairs and think that despite our numerous problems we still live in the best of times, at the end of history so to speak.

Yet our society was not always organized this way. There was a time in which the church was truly a political body that integrated every aspect of life under itself. In such a society, every good endeavor, whether it be studying or working, would have fallen under the auspices of the church. As such, most activities were imbued with meaning and purpose, to the greater service of God. The church then was more than just a country club that met on Sundays. It provided justice, education, healthcare, welfare, and even protection, though in imperfect ways.

I am fully aware that it is easy to romanticize the past when in reality such a way of organization was overladen with problems. A clarification here is overdue. I am not proposing here that we go back to a Constantinian church, a form of theocracy in which the church was in control. Such an arrangement would not be possible at this point, nor would it be beneficial to society. History has sufficiently shown that those in power always end up abusing it. The church was certainly no exception to this, though I find it questionable that nation-states and even corporations have done any better overall. But like I've said, even if not in control, the church can still be an outpost, a colony that exemplifies the right politics within the world at large. As such, it would not overturn the ways of the world by violent means, but would rather welcome outsiders to be a part of a better politics.

Though reminiscing about the past is not the goal, yet I think it important to review the history of the church and ancient Israel. This is not to imitate deed by deed what the church did in the past, but to open our imaginations to see that a different way of configuring society is not only possible but also biblical. Reviewing church history consists in part in examining the traditions of the church. As a Protestant, I do not think that every church tradition is to be followed to the letter. Yet the advantage that Catholics have is that because of their reverence for the saints past and present, they do not go about reinventing the wheel every time they start a new parish. Consider that the Apostles' Creed, which most Protestants also ascribe to, says, "I believe . . . in the holy catholic church, in the communion of saints." Those saints are saints past and present, and in order to be in communion with those of the past, as a truly universal church would, one must consider the traditions they passed down to us. This chapter then will look at the Scriptures and the history of ancient Israel and the church to find that in the past Israel and the church were indeed a robust politics, and not merely a social club or therapist. By doing so, this chapter will provide the theological foundations for recovering the sense that the church is our true political body.

THE POLITICS OF ANCIENT ISRAEL

Ancient Israel was obviously a political entity given that it was a nation. Yet it was not a nation-state in the modern sense of the word. Scriptures attest to its origins first as a family clan and then as a theocracy that was in covenantal relationship with God. Abraham is considered the patriarch or founding father of Israel. God called Abraham (then known as Abram), and made a covenant with him, a contract so to speak, to make him into a great nation out of which all peoples on Earth would be blessed (Gen 12:2–3). This was a remarkable promise given that Abram's wife, Sarai, was barren and way past the age of bearing children. All Abram was asked to do in return was to believe and trust God and eventually to circumcise himself and his sons as a sign of the covenant (Gen 17:10–14). Abram showed himself to be unfaithful to God on numerous occasions, perhaps foreshadowing Israel's unfaithfulness at times. Yet once the covenant was made, God was faithful to God's end of the bargain, giving Abraham a son from which the nation of Israel descended from. Though God kept the covenant, this never meant that Abraham had the liberty to live as he pleased in "pursuit of happiness," whatever that means. Instead, God gave Abraham the toughest of tests by asking him to sacrifice that very son whom God had given him. It is only after Abraham passed this test that God affirmed the covenant, this time by swearing to him that it would surely come to pass (Gen 22:15).

Generations later the people of Israel was formed within the context of a common bondage of slavery in Egypt. But God called them out of slavery by mighty deeds and made another covenant with them. According to Rob Barret, the book of Deuteronomy is a nation-founding document containing such a covenant, thus a political document at its core, much like the Constitution is for the United States.[90] Yet the document is focused on covenant with God rather than between the people. Israel was a chosen people that were to be God's treasured possession. As such they were to keep not only the Ten Commandments, but were to maintain justice among themselves and compassion for the most vulnerable. Of special concern were the sojourners, widows, and orphans. God made it a point to remind the people that they once were sojourners in Egypt and should therefore not oppress sojourners. They had to remember that at any point one's family could also become widows or orphans, requiring compassion from the community (Exod 22:21–24). This led to the formation of a welfare system in which the people were commanded not to harvest the edges of their fields or to gather up all their fallen grapes. They were to leave them for the poor and the immigrant among them (Lev 19:9–10). They were also not to charge interest on loans, for that would have been oppressive to the poor (Exod 22:25).

Because Israel was a politics, the authorities were not merely event planners or therapists. They actually administered justice by settling disputes among the people (Exod 18). Offerings to the temple were therefore not merely voluntary, though a few were, but mandatory (Lev 1–9). As such, offerings were taxes paid to a governing body. Consider how this stands in stark contrast to our attitudes today towards giving to the church. On average, church members in America give less than 3 percent of their income to the church, when traditionally the tithe called for 10 percent.[91] And who can blame them given that the church doesn't do much for them? After all, most people are not in need of a therapist on a weekly basis. Welfare to the poor is provided mostly by the government and non-profits more so than the church, so there are many Christians who would rather give to a non-profit of their choice rather than give the full 10 percent to the church. And apparently in acquiescence to the diminished role of the church, some pastors even encourage this form of split giving. This is the end result of none other than the church losing a sense that it is a politics.

Going back to the biblical stories of Israel's origins, what they go to show is the nature of the covenantal relationship upon which the polity of Israel was founded. This stands in sharp contrast to the social contract upon which many nation-states have been founded on. The biblical covenant was a contract between God and the people, whereas the social contract was a contract just among the people with no inclusion of God even on the sidelines. God demanded justice from the people, for that was the way God had dealt with them. On the other hand, the social contract exacts justice from individuals only to the extent that individual's rights are respected. As long as this requirement is fulfilled, one can do whatever one pleases. It is to be noted that John Locke, one of the earliest proponents of individual rights, was a libertarian of sorts. Even though there is a Christian basis for individual rights, as was discussed before, if such is the foundation of a given polity, how exactly is social welfare to be cared for? What obliges someone to be concerned of and take care of the vulnerable around him? As long as everybody's basic rights are being met, why should one be so concerned? One is therefore at liberty to accumulate vast amounts of wealth if that is what makes one "happy." On the other extreme, a democracy can also easily lead to a tyranny of the majority in which 51 percent oppress 49 percent by exerting their will upon them. Or once in a while it's the other way around, as many liberals may have felt after 2016. But a polity that has God as Lord would be one that habituates a people's desires towards the right worship of God, to love God and neighbor, not to pursue one's unrestrained desires.

This of course doesn't mean that Israel was always faithful to God. Israel broke the covenant numerous times by falling into idolatry repeatedly.

As we read about their continuous failures, it is easy for us moderns to scoff at them. What made them so obtuse that they bowed the knee to a stone or wood figure again and again? But in the ancient mind, idols were deeply political and therefore economic as well. Gods were believed to be attached to a particular location and often to a group of people. If a particular group fared well either militarily or economically, it was usually attributed to their gods. As many of the Israelites were a ragtag group of former slaves, they no doubt were seduced by the idols of stronger Canaanite groups around them. Consider the case of the Canaanite god Ba'al, who was a stumbling block for many an Israelite. Ba'al was one believed to control the rain, which was needed to grow crops and therefore to be prosperous (1 Kgs 17–18). Israel no doubt worshipped Ba'al in order to be as prosperous as some Canaanites around them. But according to the Law, any form of idolatry was political treason against their God, YHWH, who delivered them from their enemies and provided for them.[92] It's interesting how modern people are repulsed at the religious intolerance of ancient Israel, yet they would find little scruples with their own modern nation punishing its citizens for treason.

Due to their constant unfaithfulness to God's covenant, the Israelites were sent into exile to Babylon, which later was absorbed by Persia. Being in a foreign land some compromised their Jewish customs in order to blend in with the dominant empire.[93] But those who were faithful maintained an alternative politics against the empire. Some resisted the empire with violence, as was the case with the Maccabean Revolt. But others, as described in the book of Daniel, resisted the empire with prayer, fasting, and teaching, being faithful to the covenant to the point of death. Though there is no violence in Daniel's actions or his friends', the book of Daniel is regarded by many scholars as literature of resistance to empire.[94] Such faithfulness could have only been possible by maintaining faithfulness to the story of Israel, which was reinterpreted through an apocalyptic framework provided by new revelation. Apocalyptic visions provide hope in a better future, at least for the righteous. When one is under persecution, one can only be faithful when one is hopeful. Though we Christians are not nearly as persecuted in America as were Daniel and his friends, our present circumstances call us to a similar faithfulness if we are to live indeed as "resident aliens" in a nation that does not share our hope.

In all this, it is interesting to note that throughout the Old Testament there is very little mention of salvation consisting of souls rising to heaven after death. God's salvation and righteousness always consisted in delivering the people of Israel in some way or another. This may have been by giving Israel peace and prosperity in the land or by delivering them from their enemies. But in almost every instance it seems as though God's salvation took place or was promised on this material Earth and not on heaven above.

THE EARTHINESS OF JESUS AND HIS TEACHINGS

The experience of exile provided the backdrop for much of the New Testament. Though Israel had been restored in some sense under the Persian Empire, they were never completely sovereign and later succumbed to Roman rule. Though some of the people had come back to their homes, they were still under the bondage of an oppressive empire. Any description of the church in the New Testament reflects those political circumstances. Thus, the politics of the early church in many ways reflect the politics of Daniel and his friends.

In line with the thesis I am arguing, according to Cavanaugh, "In the Christian theological tradition, the fulfillment of Israel is not any nation-state, but the church."[95] The church is the eschatological fulfillment of the people of Israel. Another way to put it is that the church is in some ways the continuation of the people of Israel. Though members of the church presently are not necessarily of Jewish background, the New Testaments attests that those in Christ are like adopted children of Abraham (Rom 9:8, Gal 3:26–29). This inclusion of the Gentiles is in fulfillment of numerous Old Testament scriptures, such as that all peoples on Earth will be blessed through Abraham (Gen 12:3), or that the house of God will be a house of prayer for all peoples (Isa 56:7). Because the church is the continuation of that political body known as Israel, Jesus chose specifically twelve disciples to represent the twelve tribes of Israel. The number twelve is not accidental here. We know from the gospels that Jesus actually had more followers than twelve, Mary Magdalene for instance. But twelve needed to be chosen by name to represent the twelve tribes. This symbolism was so significant that at the founding of the early church another person had to be chosen to replace Judas, who had fallen away as one of the twelve (Acts 1:15–26).

One could argue though that there is scarce mention of the church in Mark, Luke, and John. This may simply be a reflection of the church not having been established yet, or at least confirmed by Pentecost during Jesus' ministry on Earth, though the gospels were written when the church was already in full bloom. But in no way does that mean that a politics is absent in these gospels. As a matter of fact, the gospels speak of an impending kingdom of God, or one that is already here. Consider that in Mark, John the Baptist says that the kingdom of God is near (Mark 1:15). Or in Luke, Jesus says that kingdom of God is already in our midst (Luke 17:20–21). What else is the kingdom of God but an alternative politics in which God is Lord, not Caesar? If one were just forming a country club, one wouldn't call it a kingdom, for that would have drawn the ire of Roman rulers.

Among the gospels, Matthew is the only one that does use the word "church," *ekklesia* in the original Greek, and it seems to be a significant part of Matthew's theology. Perhaps that was the reason why Matthew was a favorite of the early church fathers and was placed first among the Gospels in the biblical canon. Like every gospel, there are features about Matthew that make it unique. To start with, Matthew begins his gospel with a genealogy of Jesus that links him to the story of Israel. This genealogy is divided in sections representing phases in Israel's story, and the last section has fourteen generations from the exile to Christ. Matthew is conveying here that Jesus is putting an end to the exile. In some ways, this portends a political liberation of sorts.

Matthew also has John the Baptist early on proclaiming that the kingdom of heaven is at hand (Matt 3:2). "The kingdom of heaven" is a phrase oft repeated in Matthew. When reading this, many a Christian would envisage pie in the sky or somewhere else on the edges of the universe. And one cannot blame them, for where else would the kingdom of heaven be located but . . . heaven itself? To the untrained reader, it would seem natural to assume that the kingdom of heaven is just heaven, where our souls go to rest once we die.

Yet New Testament scholars would generally hold a differing opinion on this matter. To start with, John the Baptist does say that that kingdom is *at hand*, in other words, very near. Then there are the numerous parables about the kingdom in Matthew that start like this: "The kingdom of heaven is like . . ." What's odd about them is that none of them depict fluttering angels dressed in white with halos above their heads, which is what we normally think of as present in heaven. Instead, every single one of these parables has an earthy flavor to it. For instance the kingdom of heaven is described as yeast that a woman mixed with flour, or like a sower who planted good seed. These are earthy and material stuff that people would work with on their quotidian life on Earth. Of course, one could attempt to spiritualize these parables and say that the yeast or a mustard seed merely represents the growth of God's kingdom. Maybe so. But what can one say about the parable of the weeds or the parable of the net? The parable of the weeds is the one in which a sower planted good seed and then weed started to grow among it. The servants of the sower suggested that the weed be pulled out but the master objected and decided to sort them out at the end. The parable of the net compares the kingdom of heaven to a net that catches all kinds of fish, good and bad, which eventually are also sorted out. What is striking about these parables is not just the earthliness of the stories once again, but that even though they start out by saying "the kingdom of heaven is like . . ." there seems to be some form of evil present in them. There is the weed in the first and bad fish in the second. We tend to think that heaven is a perfect place where evil has been completely eradicated. Yet the description given in these parables suggests that they refer to this side of the resurrection on this present Earth, with evil still lurking.

What then is this kingdom of heaven exactly that Matthew talks about so frequently? I would suggest that clues to this are to be found in Matthew 16 and 18. In Matthew 16 there is that famous story in which Jesus establishes his church upon Peter the rock. After Peter correctly confesses to Jesus, "You are the Messiah," Jesus then tells him something truly marvelous. He says:

> I tell you, you are Peter, and on this rock I will build my church, and the gates of Hades will not prevail against it. I will give you the keys of the kingdom of heaven, and whatever you bind on earth will be bound in heaven, and whatever you loose on earth will be loosed in heaven. (Matt 16:18–19)

A connection here is made between the church and the kingdom of heaven. By telling Peter that he will have the keys to the kingdom and that the church will be built on him, Jesus implies that the church, and not just Peter as an individual, holds the keys to the kingdom. Peter is merely the one to get things going. To hold the keys does not merely give the owner access to a place, but authority to let people in and out. Yet we know that the church is not located up above in heaven, but down here on Earth.

Many have puzzled over the meaning of the last portion of the cited text. What does it mean that whatever is loosed or bound on Earth will also be loosed or bound in heaven? Matthew 18 offers the second interpretive key. This same phrase is repeated in Matthew 18 in the teaching of how to discipline those who sin in the church. This chapter says that when someone sins, he or she should first be confronted privately. If he does not listen then one should confront him with two or three witnesses. If still unrepentant, then the matter should be brought to the church. Ultimately, if stubbornness persists, she or he should be treated as a Gentile or tax collector (Matt 18:15–17). Gentiles and tax collectors were at the time groups that were considered outsiders to the Jewish community. To put it bluntly, the last step calls for the unrepentant to be kicked out or excommunicated from the church.

Immediately after the last disciplining step is laid out, the same verse from Matthew 16 is repeated: "whatever you bind on earth will be bound in heaven, and whatever you loose on earth will be loosed in heaven" (Matt 18:18). Based on this context as well as the one regarding the keys of the kingdom in Matthew 16, the most likely meaning of this sentence is that if the church on Earth decides to forgive someone her sins, then her sins are indeed forgiven in heaven as well. (If she is bound by the church on Earth, she is also bound in heaven.) On the other hand, if the church decides not to forgive someone his sins, perhaps by excommunication, then his sins are not forgiven in heaven. (If he is loosed by the church on Earth, he is also loosed in heaven.) So to get back to the original question, for Matthew it seems that if not the kingdom of heaven itself, the church is a mirror that reflects the kingdom on Earth or it is a foretaste of heaven on Earth.

It should be noted that the church then is entrusted with awesome authority. The authority to forgive or not to forgive sins belonged exclusively to God in the Old Testament. That is why the Pharisees were indignant at Jesus when he forgave the paralyzed man (Matt 9:2–7). But Jesus, being God himself, claimed this authority and then imparted it to his church. Yet when we look at the church today, we can only be perplexed at how far removed it has come from what Jesus intended it to be. How often do we see the church acting like it actually has some authority? When is the last time one has witnessed an excommunication? On the contrary, churches go out of their way to please and appeal to existing or potential members. And what else is one to expect when people behave like they can just go to the church next block if they are not pleased with their pastor's sermon? And even if the church does attempt to discipline its members, how can it do so if any such discipline lacks teeth? What does expulsion from a social club really mean after all? Because many churches have lost the sense that they are a politics, there simply isn't much at stake when considering whether one is in or out of the community. But if there were economic issues at stake, like every real community, then the church would actually have some teeth to discipline members and raise them as people of character.

I do not want to be misunderstood here. The church has often abused its authority so that people have grown averse to its exercise of power. But in a consumerist society in which people are under the impression that they can simply choose who they become as individuals, it becomes all the more imperative to belong to a disciplining community. It is to be noted that church discipline as prescribed by Matthew 18 does not entail physical violence of any sort. Matthew 18 is a way for us to communicate better and resolve our differences without resorting to violence. This form of verbal discipline is necessary so that the church becomes a truth-telling community. Violence is often the result of pent-up anger due to a lack of means of resolution of conflicts. According to Hauerwas, the prescriptions of Matthew 18 allow for a truthful peacemaking within a community. After all, gripes that people have with each other do not simply go away by being nice on the surface to each other. Truthful confrontation becomes necessary.[96] And if matters should remain unresolved, excommunication does not simply mean sending someone to hell indefinitely, but to tell them to repent and come home.

The church being the foretaste of the kingdom fits perfectly with the Lord's Prayer, also found in Matthew. The Lord's Prayer was Jesus teaching us to pray, as it succinctly contains most things we could possibly pray for in the right order.[97] It starts by praising God first and asking for God's kingdom and will to come before asking for our grocery list of requests, which could be included under "give us this day our daily bread." It then confesses one's sins. It is striking that nowhere in this prayer is there a request that our souls make it up to heaven when we die. Yet this is precisely what many a church has focused on from the Middle Ages up to now. Though I am sure that heaven is indeed important, the Lord's Prayer has things the other way around. Jesus teaches us to pray for God's kingdom to *come down* and thus for God's will to be done *on this Earth* as it is in heaven. Those who take this prayer seriously would want to be agents of the kingdom and would ask God how they could participate in this movement of having the kingdom down on Earth.[98] This is the true mission of the church, not just sending souls up to heaven.

To top things off, there is also the argument of Jesus' resurrection. The fact that the tomb was found empty goes to show that Jesus rose in his body, not only in his spirit. The ascension was not Jesus' spirit going up to heaven, but his entire body as well. Besides, there are remarkably material aspects of Jesus' resurrection body. For instance, his wounds could be physically touched and felt by Thomas (John 20:27–28), or Jesus could even eat fish without having it just fall out to the ground (Luke 24:42–43). These are things that only a material body within space and time could do, not a ghost or spirit.

N. T. Wright illuminates the implications of believing in Jesus' bodily resurrection. To start with, our ultimate hope should not be that our souls rise up to heaven when we die. Rather, the Scriptures promise that when we follow the way of Jesus, our physical body will rise as well. Some may wonder, why might we need a physical body in heaven where we will be like the angels? But what we find from the one of the last chapters of the Bible, Revelation 21, is that God wants to restore heaven and *Earth* anew. In it we find the New Jerusalem coming down from heaven to Earth, which in many ways would be the fulfillment of the Lord's Prayer. If our physical bodies matter, then this Earth matters as well. God's intention is not for Christians to simply abandon the Earth to hell on a handbasket, thinking it is not our home anyways. The truth is that the Earth is our home at the end of the day or time. So as N. T. Wright puts it, the church's work with the local community "to foster programs for better housing, schools, and community facilities, to encourage new job opportunities..."[99] is all part of the mission of the church. It is to be noted that all of these endeavors would entail a politics, something that many a church today is sorely lacking.

THE POLITICS OF JESUS

If indeed Jesus taught the impending coming of the kingdom *on this Earth* and not just about pie in the sky, that means that he lived and taught a politics that could be practiced here on Earth. We should then resist any spiritualization of the New Testament that calls only for individual reform of our hearts and our minds, leaving much of the structures of society unchanged, business as usual. So what exactly was Jesus' politics?

Some would recognize that I borrowed the heading for this section from John Howard Yoder's seminal work on the topic. A cursory overview of his work is in order here. When speaking specifically about the politics of the person and life of Jesus, Yoder focuses mostly on Luke's gospel. Yoder first points out that Jesus' title "Son of God" is made explicit after his baptism, when a voice came from heaven saying, "You are my beloved Son." According to Yoder, this passage is alluding to Psalm 2:7. The "Son of God" in Psalm 2 was clearly referring to Israel's king, for the psalm also speaks of the "Son of God" as "the Anointed," a title used for kings in the Old Testament (Ps 2:2).[100] Even before that, during the annunciation, Mary is told that Jesus will take over the throne of his father David (Luke 1:32). So we can see that from the get-go Luke does not shy away from portraying Jesus as King, a political figure that no doubt would command people's allegiance in competition with Caesar.

Like I've said, politics is closely tied to economics. So early on in Luke, reading from the prophet Isaiah, Jesus announces that the Spirit of the Lord is upon him to bring good news to the poor, to proclaim liberty to the captives, and to proclaim the year of the Lord's favor (Luke 4:18). We tend to think that this simply means that Jesus was going to be a good therapist and miracle worker that would lift up the downcast. Though this may all be true, Yoder argues that Jesus here was in fact proclaiming that the Year of Jubilee had arrived, the year prescribed in the Old Testament in which all debts would get cancelled.[101] This is all part of the author Luke weaving in the pieces to make it clear that Jesus' life showed special concern for the poor. It's a common theme throughout the gospel. For instance, it is in Luke (not in Matthew) that Jesus is placed in a humble manger after his birth (Luke 2:7). It is in Luke that poor shepherds visit the infant Jesus (Luke 2:8–20), whereas in Matthew he is visited and lavished with expensive gifts by the wise men from the East (Matt 2:1–12). Yoder points out that Luke does not spiritualize the Beatitudes as Matthew does. For instance, in Matthew Jesus says, "Blessed are the poor in spirit," whereas in Luke, Jesus says, "Blessed are you who are poor." Matthew's version also says, "Blessed are those who hunger and thirst for righteousness," whereas Luke's version says, "Blessed are you who are hungry now" (Compare Matt 5:1–3 to Luke 6:20–21). In the same vein, the Lord's Prayer was originally meant to be read as it is: "Forgive us our debts as we forgive our debtors." Debt here actually means monetary debts and not just generic trespasses as we often recite at church.[102] According to Yoder, Luke sees financial debt as "the paradigmatic social evil."[103]

To make this point more explicit, Yoder explicates the parable of the dishonest manager. In this parable, a manager is called by his boss to account for his mismanagement. Sensing that he'll get fired, he goes about to befriend his master's debtors by cutting a significant portion of their debts. So if someone owed a hundred jugs of olive oil to the master, he would cut it down to fifty. At the end of the story, surprisingly he is commended by his boss for acting shrewdly (Luke 16:1–13). This parable has puzzled many a layperson. Didn't this person worsen his mismanagement by cutting debts owed to his master? Is Jesus advocating cheating the master out of his money? Why is this manager commended at the end, not just by his master but also by Jesus? Historical context here is needed to understand this parable. Many a peasant in Israel had been subjected to servitude due to high taxes and debt. To make matters worse, landlords contracted middlemen (our manager in the story) who sometimes collected arbitrary sums that exceeded the rents that were due to the landlord. Yoder's take on the story is that when the manager decided to cut people's debts, he was now being honest, merely collecting what the landlord expected and not pocketing any for himself. This is why Jesus said at the end when explicating the parable, "make friends for yourselves by means of dishonest wealth, so that when it is gone, they may welcome you into the eternal homes" (Luke 16:9). In acting this way, the manager gained the friendship of his former victims and became one of them. Though the manager may have lost his wealth gained from extortion, he would have gained true wealth in his newfound friends. As Yoder puts it, Jesus was teaching through this parable to practice the Jubilee.[104]

I am sure that many a reader here would object to implementing Jubilee every fifty years as prescribed by the Old Testament. It seems to run counter to our free-market instincts and this practice would probably dry up the credit market. Who in their right mind would be willing to lend to another if all debts will eventually get cancelled? But I do not want to be misunderstood here. To start with, in this chapter I am simply stating the case that Israel and Jesus had a politics with economic ramifications. I am also not advocating that we follow the Jubilee to the letter. What's more important is to translate the spirit of that law to our modern situation. In some ways, liberal democracies already follow the spirit of Jubilee through bankruptcy laws that allow debtors to be forgiven and start over when unable to repay debts. Of course, I think that a lot more could be done. But also, the argument I'm trying to press in this book is not that problems be solved through government policy, at least not primarily. What I am advocating is that the church should recognize its own political nature and therefore stake out its own microeconomic space. What this may look like will be covered in the following chapter. I will simply point out here that Yoder says, I think correctly, that if the Jubilee dispositions had been practiced every so often up to our day, many bloody revolutions would have been avoided.[105] I already said that for all the virtues of the free market, one of its main problems is that it unceasingly accumulates wealth in the hands of a few, which has often been the catalyst for bloody revolutions. So Jubilee was not a bad practice after all.

It is important to note that though Jesus taught inclusive and compassionate economic practices, Jesus never implemented his ideals through force. Nation-states have often implemented their policies, even good ones, by force. Even liberal democracies can sometimes be oppressive as the majority gets to enforce their ideals on the minority. But violence was never part of Jesus' politics. Yoder points out that the life of discipleship is that of following the nonviolent politics of Jesus. This is ultimately the crucial part about the politics of Jesus. Of course, the only way this could be done is by giving up control or power. Jesus, after all, gave up his life willingly instead of fighting back. So to follow Jesus would mean embracing his pattern of life, which includes suffering servanthood, subordination, forgiveness, and even death as victory.[106]

THE POLITICS OF THE EARLY CHURCH

A cursory overview of Acts of the Apostles reveals that the early church also had a politics based on the lordship of Christ. Jesus' lordship is in fact what the apostles were proclaiming in their preaching (Acts 2:36; 28:31). But for years many scholars believed that Luke, the author of Acts, wanted to defend Christianity as a non-threatening religion to the Roman authorities. This would explain the numerous declarations in Acts that though they were arrested multiple times, the apostles were at the end found innocent by the Roman authorities. Such was the case when the apostles stood before the Roman rulers Gallio, Lysias, Felix, and Festus (Acts 18, 21–23, 23–24, 25–26). But to focus on this aspect of Acts would give the misleading impression that since Christians focused on spiritual matters, they never really threatened Rome's earthly rule. This reading would support much of our current spiritualization of the gospel that ends up fracturing our lives. It makes us believe that the church is concerned with our soul while the nation is concerned with politics and economics, with very little clash between the two entities.

But to truly proclaim the lordship of Jesus is to say that Jesus stands above Caesar, king, or president. The lordship of Christ would leave little room for accommodation with the state when the two kingdoms come into conflict. In his commentary of Acts, Kavin Rowe points out that there is an overarching tension throughout the text between the innocence of the apostles and the fact that they were still persecuted.[107] If there were no conflict whatsoever between Christianity and the way of life of the Greeks and Romans, why were the Christians so frequently persecuted?

It is helpful here to be more specific. What exactly were the apostles accused of and later declared to be innocent of? As it turns out, they often were specifically accused of causing public unrest through their preaching. When Paul preached in Jerusalem, "the violence of the mob was so great that he had to be carried by the soldiers" (Acts 21:35). Or when Paul stood before Felix, the Jews accused him of being "an agitator among all the Jews throughout the world" (Acts 24:5). The original Greek uses the word *stasis* for "agitator." *Stasis* was a word often associated with unrest leading to sedition by the Roman Empire. Roman governors were entrusted with their position to keep the peace in their province and any public unrest was dealt with seriously, especially in Palestine, which was notoriously unruly.[108] It is against this charge that Paul defends himself. Since he was simply preaching peacefully and it is the unbelieving Jews themselves that caused the unrest, the Roman authorities couldn't find a basis to charge him and found him innocent. So the reason why the apostles were often declared innocent at the end of their trial is not that their worldview and way of life did not clash with that of the Romans. It is simply that they were not responsible for the public unrest. This repeated innocence of the apostles simply goes to show that Christians were not out there to violently depose or take over the state, not that there wasn't a disruption of life brought about by the gospel.[109] Though Jesus is Lord, the church's politics is not dependent on a coup d'état.

So how exactly does the proclamation of Jesus' lordship upend the politics, culture, and economics wherever introduced? To start with, religious belief is at the center of every cultural system. In Acts, the apostles were simply proclaiming everywhere they went that Jesus is Lord and all other gods are not. This straightforward proclamation led to the disruption of local economies and concentrations of power. For example, when Paul and his companions exorcised a spirit of divination out of a slave girl in Philippi, her owners were upset because their income from her divination skills had dried out. So the crowd attacked the apostles, beat them, and put them in jail (Acts 16:16–40). On another occasion, the people of Ephesus were upset because many of their artisans made a living from selling silver shrines of their deity Artemis. So they organized a riot chanting, "Great is Artemis of the Ephesians!" and brought Paul and his companions to be judged by the authorities (Acts 19:21–41). Clearly, by the simple preaching of the gospel economies were disrupted and local big shots lost their power and prestige.

If economics is a projection of our priorities, it will naturally mirror our religious beliefs. Imagine if Christians really practiced what they preached. Then businesses like Bentley or Louis Vuitton would have to close down for lack of demand. If that ever happened, should we feel pity for their employees and therefore prop up those businesses? That is the way of thinking of many a free-market advocate and becomes an excuse for lavish spending. But we shouldn't think this way. I'm sure that those talented employees could find more meaningful jobs than alleviating the insecurities of the wealthy. That would naturally be the case if demand became more properly allocated towards the real needs of people.

Another feature of the book of Acts is that it portrays the church as the body of Christ. Thus, the church in Acts undergoes and performs almost exactly the same things that Jesus did and experienced. For instance, the church breaks bread, performs baptisms, preaches, prays, heals, takes care of those in need, and because of it all gets persecuted even to the point of death. Like Jesus, like church. If we were to compare the church today in the West with the church in Acts, we would find that our churches collectively undergo many of the things that the early church did, at least to some meager degree. But there is one glaring missing item. On the most part, the Western church today lacks persecution. Now I'm not suggesting that Christians should go out there and try to get intentionally persecuted. Though God values martyrs, I don't think it would please God to have oneself killed on purpose. But lack of persecution perhaps reveals that something is not quite right with the church today. Could it be a symptom of the church accommodating too much to the world? Has the church grown too comfortable becoming an agent of the state, merely helpful in raising good moral citizens for the nation?

But the early church was persecuted precisely because its politics and way of life was so counter and offensive to the life of the unbelievers it encountered. That was the cause of so much unrest. For instance, "all who believed were together and had all things in common; they would sell their possessions and goods and distribute the proceeds to all, as any had need" (Acts 2:44–45). This took place at the very beginning stages of the nascent church. As the church grew rapidly, a more organized welfare was systematized. Some in the church complained that their widows were being neglected in the daily distribution of food. As a result, a select group was chosen to make sure that resources got to those most in need while the apostles devoted themselves to prayer and serving the word (Acts 6:1–7). Like I've said, a genuine community is one where members have economic commitments to each other, often costly. In the Roman world, where power was concentrated at the top and the poor were often neglected, the church provided a place where the hungry were filled and the sick received healing. Yet how many churches put this into practice nowadays? Today we just expect the government to provide welfare and healthcare while we just go to church to hang out. Like I've said, we have let the state take over many of the roles that the church pioneered.

The story of Ananias and Sapphira should serve here as a cautionary tale to us all. They were apparently a wealthy couple that wanting to join the early community, and they brought a portion of their possessions to the apostles while pretending to offer everything they had. They were both struck dead by God on the spot (Acts 5:1–11). This story no doubt offends our modern sensibilities. Shouldn't they have been rewarded for their willingness to join the church and their giving a portion of their wealth? Isn't that what basically all of us Christians do today? Don't people have a right to keep at least part of their hard-earned money? This story would no doubt be compunctious to preach from for many a pastor. It is certainly so for me to write about it as well. But I think, at its heart, this story challenges the American lie that my money is mine because I earned it and therefore I can spend it in any way I want. Ultimately, everything we possess, including our material wealth, came from God and thus belongs to God. Perhaps because of our unwillingness to acknowledge this, the church is experiencing a death of some sort.

I do not know exactly what it would look like for the church today to practice fellowship the way it did at its inception. But in his lectures, Hauerwas has suggested that the church, or at least its pastor, should know how much money each person in the congregation makes and has. Once again, this may offend our modern sensibilities since we tend to think that finances are a personal matter. But only when such knowledge is public can those in authority go to those who have a lot and ask that they give for those who are in need. Inequality is often exacerbated by the ignorance of those at the bottom of the ladder. They know that the rich have more money than them, but they are often clueless as to the extent of the disparity. If they really knew just how rich are the rich, there probably would be more frequent revolts. If it sounds outrageous that church authorities know about members' finances, how is it that we provide all this information to the Internal Revenue Service? Once again, we have the tendency to think that America is of weightier importance than the church.

Many will object here that socialism simply does not work. I would agree. History has sufficiently shown that it has been fatal for millions. It simply does not work when a secular state tries to impose this system without taking into account the necessary moral formation for this system to even have a chance. But whether we say we believe in it or not, there is one place in which all of us practice socialism and it actually works! It is no other than the social unit we call the family. Within a family, each member is asked to contribute according to their abilities and they are allowed to take according to their needs. Parents often do not split their resources in a meritocratic manner among their children. If one child is sick while the other one is healthy, parents will pour more of their resources in helping the sick child. The famous parable of the prodigal son illustrates well a parent's heart towards his or her children. Even if one child squanders all his wealth, he is still welcomed back in the house to share at the same table with his more responsible brother. Socialism works in the family not only because it is small, but also because there is moral discipline and formation infused with love. Where such moral formation fails, even family is forced to cut ties.

The remarkable thing though is that family came to acquire a new meaning among Christians. On one occasion when Jesus was teaching, his mother and brothers came to him. But he retorted, "Who is my mother and who are my brothers?" And pointing to his disciples, he said, "Here are my mother and my brothers!" (Matt 12:48–49). This story does make Jesus look like an irreverent punk. Who would say that about his mother? But what Jesus was doing was to reconfigure the family to include the church. Consider that on another occasion Jesus said:

> For I have come to set a man against his father,
> and a daughter against her mother,
> and a daughter-in-law against her mother-in-law;
> and one's foes will be members of one's own household.
>
> Whoever loves father or mother more than me is not worthy of me; and whoever loves son or daughter more than me is not

worthy of me; and whoever does not take up the cross and follow me is not worthy of me. (Matt 10:34–38).

So much for family values. But what Jesus was essentially saying is that the church is more constitutive for human relationships than the family! This is the reason why in many churches people call each other "brother" and "sister." Often times people say these words with sentimentality, a nice feeling of having such a big and happy family to hang out with. But we must remember that family is family because of economic commitments to each other. We are not closer to family because we get along best with its members. Families often have numerous disagreements. But family is family because, at the end of the day, members take care of each other. So when Jesus reconfigured the family to be the church, that's exactly what he expects and that is exactly what the church in Acts did. I will elaborate on what I think this should look like today in the next chapter.

THE POLITICS OF THE MEDIEVAL CHURCH

At the time that the New Testament was penned, the church was a persecuted minority within the Roman Empire, albeit a rapidly growing one. It continued to be so for a few hundred years. But there was a profound shift around the year 312 AD, when the Roman Emperor Constantine converted to Christianity. Suddenly, Christianity went from being a persecuted to a tolerated religion. Then a few decades later Christianity became the official religion of the empire, going from tolerated to finally being a religion persecuting of surrounding pagan beliefs. Some scholars call this the Constantinian shift or they call a church in power the Constantinian church.

Many of the dynamics of what it meant to be church surely changed then. Suddenly there was no distinction between church and the world. If you were born within the empire, you were baptized and you were a Christian by default. There still was a "world" out there, but they were the ones outside the confines of the empire, such as the Muslims. This thorough inversion of power no doubt led to many grievous errors by the church. The bloody Crusades are but one example of the numerous abuses that took place with the church at the helm. The crimes of the church are too many to count and it is beyond the present scope of this book to go through all of them. These have been exhaustively documented by historians elsewhere.

But though most of the errors of the church are inexcusable, I do think it important to put them into perspective. About a century after Christianity became the official religion of Rome, the empire collapsed in 476 AD. As the barbarians attacked, the church was seen as the surviving and viable political institution and so it was that the church took on that role. Suddenly people looked to the church to provide basic things such as justice, welfare, and protection, and since the barbarians did not initially have the most established of institutions, the church stepped into that role. The problem then was that the church became no different from any other violent state. When reviewing church history, people are often shocked that the church would lead people into murderous wars. Yet people are not shocked at all to find kings or nation-states behaving violently, since it is all they did in the past. This double standard arises from the failure to see the church as a state at in those times. But it is important to recognize that the church was simply behaving like any other of its contemporaneous states. This of course doesn't make its deeds or the deeds of any other state excusable. They were all an equally rotten bunch. It is mostly the double standard that the church is treated with that I am against.

For years, people have often derided the Middle Ages as the "Dark Ages," with the finger pointed squarely at the church. But this is a gross mischaracterization of Christians. The term "Dark Ages" was used to refer to the general decline of civilization at the time compared to the advancements of Rome. Yes, it is true that the church was in some respects groping in the dark, as was everyone else. But to set the record straight, civilization initially declined as a direct result of the fall of Rome, not the rise of the church. As a matter of fact, as the surviving political entity after Rome's fall, the church was in many ways the glue that held things together when the world was falling apart. The church provided care for the sick and founded schools, which eventually led to the rise of the first universities.

It is easy to pinpoint and focus on all the errors of the church. But for the purposes of this book, I would like to point out that the church had a politics at the time. It may have been the wrong politics altogether, but at the very least the church had one, whereas one can barely find any today. What that meant is that the church integrated all the various aspects of peoples' lives under one unified whole. There wasn't a disjunction like we have today between one's work, one's family life, and the church. Every field of study was also integrated with theology, which was known as the queen of the sciences. This is where I think church tradition can provide invaluable insights. If the church is truly the communion of saints past and present, this means that there is much to be learned from the medieval church, even with all its blunders. I will thus explore each of the above strands in more detail in the following sections.

THE CHURCH, THE ECONOMY, AND INDUSTRY

I've already pointed out that from the get-go the church had an overtly distinct economy from that of the Roman Empire. For two millennia now, monasteries have faithfully picked up and carried on that same counter-cultural spirit. The monastic movement started off with people fleeing to the desert from the Roman way of life. As such, they were people who renounced the riches and material comforts of the world around them. Many were initially isolated hermits but as they acquired a growing number of followers, they found the need to organize themselves into monastic life.

It wasn't only in their poverty vows and communal life that monasteries were different. Most had a regimented schedule of prayer, study, and work. Consider the Rule of Saint Benedict, which states, "Idleness is the enemy of the soul. The brethren, therefore, must be occupied at stated hours in manual labour . . . for then are they truly monks when they live by the labour of their hands, like our fathers and the apostles."[110] The last part clearly shows that though monks valued the work of their hands, they were not introducing an innovation. This is exactly what Paul or his followers meant many years before when the Scriptures say, "Anyone unwilling to work should not eat" (2 Thess 3:10). Though those in the early church and the monasteries shared their possessions freely, this was not tolerated as an excuse for idleness.

All of this ran completely counter to the values of the empire. Though initially Romans had started off as ordinary farmers, their labor was replaced as the empire added vast numbers of slaves from conquered peoples. In the last five centuries of Roman history, there was about one slave for every two or three Roman citizens.[111] As slaves started to take on the dirty work, Romans despised manual labor as not worthy of a free person. It was to the extent that even the renowned Roman orator Cicero said:

> Gentlemen should not soil themselves with means of livelihood which provoke ill-will . . . Degrading and vulgar also are the gains of all hired workmen whom we pay for manual labour . . . because their wages are the very badge of servitude. All mechanics are occupied in a degrading way, for no workshop can have anything about it worthy of a free man.[112]

We can see why the ways of the early church and the monasteries must have been repulsive to many a Roman. While Romans valued leisure and luxury, monasteries flipped Roman values on its head by elevating dirty work.

On the issue of slavery, the church has always played an important role in all abolitionist movements throughout history. Such was the case in Rome, the British Empire, and America. But the church never attained this goal by means of violent revolt. Early on, Paul preached that in Christ "there is no longer slave or free" (Gal 3:28). Paul also pleaded to a fellow Christian to release a slave, counting the slave as a "beloved brother" to his master as well as to Paul (Phlm 16). Traditional Roman hierarchies no longer applied to those whom Christ had set free. The church thoroughly upended Roman values on their head. And ultimately, if the Christian economy did not necessitate slaves because everyone was to work side by side, why would a Christian keep his or her slaves around?

But going back to the monasteries, if monks were frugal and worked hard, what economic outcome should we expect over time? As it turns out, the accumulation of capital would eventually lead to further improvements in the form of investments in industry. Does this start to sound a bit like capitalism? It should indeed. According to Randall Collins, Max Weber's famous thesis that the Protestant ethic started capitalism is mistaken in a sense. It actually started much earlier through the monasteries.[113]

There are numerous cases that illustrate this point. While money could not easily move from one feudal land to another during medieval times, the church provided a way to do this as it was the only international organization in Europe. Many Augustinian houses functioned as banks, as they were taking deposits and investing the money.[114] Where exactly was this money invested? The constant and arduous manual labor of monasteries eventually led them to improve their work through the development of industry and machinery. We tend to think that industry suddenly started with the Industrial Revolution in Britain during the 1800s, but the seeds of it had been scattered here and there throughout the church. For instance, Cistercian monasteries were in fact well-organized factories, as they used water-powered mills to produce wheat and textiles.[115] They were also the leading iron producers, which was employed not only for more machinery, but in clearing vast lands for agriculture. They produced so much that they sold their surplus, and the profits could then go back for reinvestment.[116] The Cistercians also produced lead, copper, zinc, and silver.[117] This was not the case with just a few Cistercian monasteries though. They implemented their machinery and regimented labor schedules wherever they could, so in fact the Cistercians were very much like an international corporation. Their footprint was so noticeable that it prodded other forms of economic development, such as its investment practices.[118] The church was therefore the most dynamic economic sector in Europe at the time.[119]

In regards to labor, while medieval feudalism did not allow for much vertical mobility, the church freely recruited from all social ranks. Anyone could join the ranks of the church regardless of social class. But recruitment was not limited to monks only and the church did not pay miserly wages to church outsiders for its time. In the years 1300–1305, the workmen that built the spire of the Church of Bonlieu-en-Forez had cheese, meat, wine, bread, and bean soup to eat.[120] Not a bad meal for someone living in medieval times.

The point that I'm trying to make is not just that the church was an economic powerhouse that contributed to people's material well-being. It's that, and also that the church at its heart integrated work with faith. If one worked for the Cistercians or any other church organization, one knew that one was contributing to the work of the church. For them, work was more meaningful than simply making a buck. This was far better than having a feudal lord (or a CEO in modern times) make most of the profit for selfish use. Sure enough the church didn't always use its wealth for the greater good. Though monks could not own wealth individually, the church was at times infamous for its institutional wealth.[121] It often used part of it to make grandiose cathedrals. But much of this wealth was also used for charity that benefited local communities, as will be shown in the next sections.

Yet people today tend to think that the church should have no involvement in economic matters as it would hinder economic efficiency and growth. An example that is often paraded around is that of usury laws. For much of Christian history, the church prohibited the collection of interests made on loans between Christians, based on the same prescription of Leviticus 25:36. We moderns think this is a silly law, for to implement it would completely dry up the credit markets. Who would be willing to lend if no profit can be made from the loan? Perhaps the church did enforce this law mindlessly sometimes, but we should not miss the spirit behind this prescript. Today, it is the wealthy and the corporations who borrow most from the banks. They do so on the most part to fund an investment or a business. But most banks in the West simply do not loan money to a poor person for fear that they will not repay their loan. So it is right for the bank to charge interest on the money given that most loans are made to the well-off. In the ancient past, on the other hand, it was mostly the poor who needed to borrow money, sometimes just to get by. In dire circumstances, the only other option was to sell oneself or one's family into slavery. Therefore, to charge interest on a loan made to a desperate person would have been just heartless. So Leviticus had it right all along. Unfortunately this practice still takes place in the form of payday loans that charge exorbitant interest rates to those who are most vulnerable. Can we really say that there should not be any regulation whatsoever on these businesses? Our present economic systems may have changed from that of the past, but the same spirit of Leviticus should apply.

Another way in which the church meddled in economic affairs was by arbitrating discussions on just prices. Is there a fair price for any particular good or labor? If a merchant charged too much for an item, was she or he behaving unjustly? This was a contentious issue during medieval times, and certainly not one that was settled or enforced heavily.[122] We moderns tend to think that supply and demand alone, and not morality of any sort, should determine the price of a good. Generally I agree with this position and there were many in the Middle Ages that did as well. But there are times when the concept of a just price does apply. Was it not outrageous when the price of EpiPens used for those with severe allergies suddenly shot upwards from $100 to $600? Is there really no such thing as morality in prices? Doesn't the incessant escalating price of healthcare in America show that some form of moral intervention needs to take place?

THE CHURCH AND EDUCATION

Because the vast majority of people today send their kids to a public school, we tend to think that education is and should be provided by the state. But that was not exactly how educational institutions as we know them originated in the West. Though the church was in no way the progenitor of the first schools, it played a significant role in continuing and improving education after the fall of the Roman Empire. There are many today who deride the church as an anti-intellectual and boorish institution, sometimes with good reason. But that was certainly not the case in the past. The clergy were among the most educated men among the populace. Though that may not always be the case today, we can still see the legacy that the church has imprinted in education. Frankly, if it were not for the church, we wouldn't be where we are intellectually. After all, the church played a significant role in the formation of the first universities.

To start from the beginning, the Roman state supported a series of public schools as they needed an educated bureaucracy for their constantly expanding empire. These schools taught mostly grammar and rhetoric while much of the other schooling happened at home.[123] But as the Roman Empire crumbled, the church gradually took over this role. The state lacked the funding for schools and there was less need for educating imperial bureaucrats.[124] As Christianity grew though, some Christians became educated to the extent that many became clerical teachers, teaching secular subjects in these schools.[125]

Not only did those Roman schools morphed into schools that were religious in character, but monasteries also played an important role in educating the public. Saint Benedict's Rule did not only prescribe work, but also devoted times for "sacred reading."[126] The church by nature incentivized literacy, as Christians are a people of the Book. Though literacy did not become widespread among the laity until after the printing press was invented, at least those who devoted themselves to the service of God had an incentive to learn how to read in order to study the Scriptures. Monasteries in particular democratized learning as these were not just available to the wealthy, but any who wanted to join. As monasteries developed and expanded their reach, they did not only read and teach the Bible, but also became more systematic schools that taught a wide variety of subjects such as the church fathers, Homer, Virgil, architecture, carving, metallurgy, music, and classical languages.[127]

The widening of Christianity throughout Europe had the effect of spreading education wherever it went. For instance, the Slavic alphabet was created to facilitate the spread of Christianity among its people.[128] Also, the Dominicans made great efforts to educate their preachers because they believed that this fostered more effective preaching.[129] They eventually came to see studying as a penitential discipline, as a means of sanctification.[130] Because of this emphasis on education, they often sent their own to the nascent universities, and as such they became one of their patrons. Their most famous member was of course Thomas Aquinas.[131]

Speaking of higher education, perhaps the most significant contribution of the Middle Ages to our times was the formation of the first universities. Today's highest academic institutions are a legacy of this era. One of course cannot say that the church alone contributed to the formation of the first universities, for these were the product of kings, townspeople, students, and the church coming together. Nevertheless, the church played a central role. That theology was known as the queen of the sciences goes to show the Christian origins of the university. The church as a whole, not just its monasteries and individual orders, but from its very top, supported the university because it needed to defend a rationally intelligible doctrine.[132] The church sent some of its members to study at the universities, leading to an educated clergy at the top. By the thirteenth century, popes themselves had usually attended a university and they usually surrounded themselves with educated cardinals.[133] By comparison, though most of today's church leaders have also attended some form of higher education, things are quite different as Silicon Valley and Wall Street end up snatching the best and brightest.

What then was the academic ethic at the medieval university? What was presupposed in medieval thought to foster this type of learning? As it turns out, religious belief was at the bottom of it all. According to Walter Ruegg, the medieval university was ultimately the product of "the belief in a world order, created by God, rational, accessible to human reason, to be explained by human reason."[134] Without such belief in a rational order set up by God, there would be no reason for scientific study. Science, after all, presupposes consistency in nature, and if one believed that God were whimsical, there would be no reason for the study of science. Also, the belief in human beings as fallen creatures led to a culture of intellectual criticism and collegial cooperation. After all, scholars could debate each other at the medieval university. Yet at the same time, there was belief in the human potential for scientific inquiry based on the credo that we are made in God's image. In addition, most of the knowledge produced by the university was eventually made public due to the belief that scholarly knowledge was a public good and ultimately a gift from God.[135]

The point is that knowledge used to be integrated by the church into one coherent worldview. People didn't study philosophy, history, law, or science as though those subjects had nothing in common with theology. The church, more than the state, played an integral role in providing literacy and educating vast numbers of people, and thus there was moral formation in it. Today the opposite is the case, as the state is expected to provide education. But when a secular state that claims moral neutrality is the main provider, knowledge cannot but become fractured. Perhaps of all academic subjects, the natural sciences are the ones that have become most distanced from religious belief. But in the next section I will show that those who advanced science at the medieval university were deeply motivated by their religious beliefs.

THE CHURCH AND SCIENCE

Many people today believe that the church is an anti-intellectual institution that refuses to accept scientific findings. To our embarrassment, this certainly is the case sometimes. Arguably, the three most notorious instances that are often paraded around are: when Galileo was told to recant his astronomical findings by the church authorities; the Scopes Monkey Trial, which was a public school teacher put on trial for teaching evolution; and the last one is currently unfolding as numerous Christian policy makers refuse to accept the latest scientific consensus on the warming of the planet due to human activities. However, to simply deride the church as anti-intellectual based on these errors would be grossly unfair. To start with, the fact that there have been so many philosophical debates regarding the existence of God goes to show that the possibility of God's existence cannot be rationally thrown out so easily. Second, as stated in the previous section, the church provided the environment for the creation of universities and much of scientific advancement would not have happened without the church. When one looks at the historical record, the church supported science more often than not, as I hope to make clear in this section.

In *The Genesis of Science*, James Hannam states that those who advanced science did so because they believed in the consistent character of God, whose created natural world would reflect his character. For instance, in the twelfth century, William of Conches tried to reconcile Genesis 1 with natural philosophy and was a believer in consistent natural laws that reflected God's character.[136] Later on, Thomas Aquinas postulated that the world was subject to cause and effect. Because things behaved in predictable ways, it was worth studying the causes of those things.[137] And study them they did. Hannam has an exhaustive list of scientific and technological contributions of the Middle Ages, all motivated by religious beliefs, of which I will only mention a few.

Richard of Wallingford studied at Oxford and was supported by the Benedictines. He created a mechanical clock, which was then used to guide the regimented schedule of monasteries.[138] Also, many attribute Nicolaus Copernicus to have come up with the first heliocentric model of the universe, with the sun at the center rather than the Earth. But he could not have done this on his own. The reality is that he built on the thoughts and research of many other medieval scholars. For instance, before Copernicus, John Buridan suggested that the Earth might be turning. The Greeks had thought that the entire universe turned full circle each day, but to Buridan that seemed highly inefficient and improbable, a design not fitting that of an elegant God.[139] It is to be noted here that the Greeks, who were highly respected during the Middle Ages, had proposed a geocentric model of the universe, one in which the Earth stood at the center. But Buridan challenged widely accepted Aristotelian beliefs on motion. For instance, Aristotle had postulated that everything that moves is being moved by something or someone else. But is a thrown ball continuously moving in the air due to a constant spiritual force applied to it? Aristotle didn't understand that moving things have inertia. Buridan called it "impetus," which in some ways was his own understanding of inertia. To Buridan, planets could continuously move without spirits moving them because God had endowed each one of them with their own impetus at the moment of creation.[140] With this new understanding of impetus, Buridan's disciple Nicole Oresme, who also happened to be a bishop, could provide an answer to those who challenged him on his belief of the rotating Earth. Why would an arrow shot straight up fall straight down if the Earth is indeed rotating, they would argue. But of course we know that the arrow has the "impetus" of the rotating Earth itself and so falls straight down even if the Earth is rotating.[141]

Those that deride the medieval times as "Dark Ages" assume that the predominant thought of the time, scholasticism, never challenged the ancient Greeks, who were often wrong regarding scientific matters. But this was clearly not so, as in the case of Buridan and Oresme. We tend to think that the scholastics were always backwards because of their unquestioning respect towards the ancients, but in many respects it was the humanists later on who were dogmatic. In the sixteenth century, the Renaissance brought such contempt for scholasticism that Oxford University sold off its bookcases. Merton College handed over 900 manuscripts to bookbinders to cut them up to be reused for newly printed book covers.[142]

At the same time, we shouldn't assume that scientists working from the sixteenth century onward had discarded their devotion to God. Copernicus's scientific research was highly motivated by his faith in God. In postulating that the sun was at the center of the universe, he wanted to provide a model worthy of its Creator, whom he called "the best and most orderly workman of all."[143] The same was true for Johannes Kepler, who also put the sun at the center of the universe. He also believed that the heavens had to reflect the perfection of its Creator.[144] Myriads of other examples could be provided of devout religious scientists who made great contributions to our body of knowledge. One simply has to look at the historical record to find out that many a great scientist was a priest, bishop, monk, or nun, a Christian in some form or another.

What then can be said about some of the embarrassing cases I mentioned at the beginning of this section? Galileo's trial is paraded as an example in which the church suppressed science. Galileo had defended the Copernican heliocentric system but was told to recant or face the Inquisition. What the church did here was clearly inexcusable. But it would be erroneous to view Galileo's trial as the result of a monolithic institution that was out there to quash science. In many ways, Galileo's trial was the result of the personal flaws of the pope at that time, Urban VIII, not of the church as an institution. Urban believed that he had come to power due to preordained astrological conjectures.[145] It is to be noted that just because people were discovering that the Earth moved around the sun, this doesn't mean that astrology disappeared immediately. It was certainly a gradual transition from astrology to astronomy, and many that we today respect as astronomers still retained many astrological beliefs. Urban had actually started in cordial terms with Galileo and at one point personally explained to him his position about the cosmological debate. He believed that no matter what mathematical models people came up with, it was beyond man's understanding to understand how the celestial bodies really worked.[146] When Galileo later published his famous *Dialogue*, he put the erroneous geocentric view in the mouth of Simplicio, a character in his book that is made to look plain stupid. When the pope read it, he was furious, for he must have seen it as a personal attack on his own intelligence.[147] Ultimately, that's why Galileo was brought to trial. It was all because the pope was wrong about an issue and wanted to save face. We cannot judge the entire church as anti-intellectual based on this isolated incident. Why, for instance, were Copernicus and Kepler not brought to trial if they held the same views as Galileo?

As for the Scopes Monkey Trial, it certainly was highly publicized on purpose. The trial came to symbolize the growing divide between fundamentalists and modernists. Fundamentalism was in many ways an overreaction to some of the liberal methods of inquiry introduced in the seminaries that originated from the Enlightenment. This repulsion of modernism was understandable given that not all Enlightenment ideas were to be embraced, as we are finding out today. It's just that people often overreact, as history abundantly shows. But here once again, one cannot claim that the entire church is fundamentalist. Perhaps a larger portion of the church than we wish has fundamentalist beliefs, but in no way are they the church's representatives. Critics of fundamentalists often think that Christians have always been so and dismiss religion altogether as boorish. But many ancients did not read Genesis literally as fundamentalists do. As a matter of fact, many scholars in the ancient past read the Scriptures allegorically. Fundamentalism, like I said, is actually a very modern phenomenon and the entirety of the church does not deserve to be tainted by it.

The most recently embarrassing case of course is that of Christian policy makers who deny the reality of climate change due to human activities. Once again though, these politicians do not represent the church as a whole. If anything, they show what happens when Christians are overly invested in the nation-state as their primary polity. At the end of the day, those politicians are the product of the two-party system of U.S. politics which leads to polarizing worldviews. Big businesses that benefit from denying climate change usually support the Republican Party. Because this party also happens to stand for moral values, many Christians are duped into supporting all things Republican, including the denial of climate change. Is this really the product of an anti-intellectual church opposed to science? Only to the degree that some church leaders are perhaps not the best and brightest. It seems to me that this is really more the product of the polarizing nature of U.S. politics.

All in all, it is sufficiently clear that the church stood for scientific advancement most of the time. Without the church, we would not be where we are today. Unfortunately, today the church has relegated this important role to the government, universities, and even private corporations. It is time that Christians think about how to recover a sense of the church as the patron of the sciences.

HEALTHCARE, WELFARE, AND THE CHURCH

In American politics, due to healthcare's rapidly escalating costs, who pays for it and manages it has become one of the most hotly contested issues. Republicans believe that healthcare is most efficiently managed by the private sector while many Democrats believe that the government should distribute costs equitably by taking over the insurance industry. In some ways, both points of view are really two sides of the same coin. At the end of the day, both sides believe that a secular amoral entity, be it the state or the free market, can best regulate and distribute the goods.

Yet healthcare was from the church's start a moral and religious task taken on by the church voluntarily. Clearly the inspiration behind this undertaking was that Jesus himself was a healer. Wherever Jesus went, people would bring the sick to him and he would take their ailments so that they would become fully participating members of society. The apostles of the early church, embodying Christ himself, also healed those in need (Acts 5:12–16). It is important to note that Jesus and the early church took care of any person in need, not just the sick. It just happened to be the case that in the past those in need were often also those who were sick. This shouldn't be surprising as one's health determined one's ability to work and support one's family. If a working family member fell ill, it could bring ruin upon the entire family. Thus the task of healing was naturally conjoined with the task of providing for the needy.

This stood in stark contrast with the pagan world. As I mentioned before, the social classes that developed in Roman society created a culture in which slaves and the needy were looked down upon. So when in the fifth century famine and plague struck the city of Edessa, "even those who were in the first stages of the disease they thrust away, and fled from their dearest. They would even cast them in the roads half-dead, and treat the unburied corpses as vile refuse, in their attempt to avoid ... contagion."[148] Yet during that same crisis, Christians behaved in a rather different way. Eusebius, bishop of Edessa, observed:

> Of our brethren in their exceeding love and affection for the brotherhood were unsparing of themselves and clave to one another, visiting the sick without a thought as to the danger, assiduously ministering to them, tending them in Christ, and so most gladly departed this life along with them; being infected with the disease from others, drawing upon themselves the sickness from their neighbours, and willingly taking over their pains. And many, when they had cared for and restored to health others, died themselves ... In this manner the best any rate of our brethren departed this life.[149]

If Christians were willing to give their lives to take care of the needy, one can only imagine how extensive the care was that they provided while alive. Women played a momentous role by voluntarily providing nursing care to the sick, which in turn led to many converts to Christianity.[150] Many of us Christians sometimes wonder why people in the past converted to Christianity in droves while today very few do so despite massive evangelism efforts. After reviewing the history, is it really any surprise?

The initial failure of the pagan state to alleviate poverty and suffering called for the systematization of healthcare and welfare by the church. Early on, the Apostolic Constitutions were set up, which normalized some established charitable practices. Church leaders were to collect alms from wealthy Christians and redistribute them to those in need. Some bishops were to even seek out the sick in their own houses, going door to door.[151] As eventually the state became a Christian state, the emperor was seen as having an obligation to do works of mercy and provide for his subjects, thus becoming a patron of charity.[152] Thus a welfare state gradually developed, including the foundation of churches, almshouses, orphanages, and hospitals.[153] The church continued to take on this important task even after the final collapse of the Roman Empire. During Merovingian times, the local bishop was required to put aside one fourth of revenues for the needs of the poor. Many in need were sheltered in what was known as a poorhouse next to the church.[154] In addition, due to their regimented schedule of labor and services, monasteries also eventually became the de facto providers of charity and medical care.[155]

Perhaps critics would argue that reports of miraculous healings are just not believable. Or they would say that medical knowledge was so backwards at the time that many of the sick were not really getting helped. The practice of bleeding patients is a case in point. Here, it must be noted that the church obviously realized early on that not every Christian had the gift of healing as some of the early apostles did. Thus, early Christian theology accepted the role of medicine in alleviating sickness. John Chrysostom, a church father, stated that medical knowledge could be acquired by studying the works of Hippocrates and Galen, ancient pagan doctors, and through apprenticeship alongside experienced doctors.[156] Even though Hippocrates and Galen were wrong on many accounts, the church's openness to them goes to show its receptiveness to the latest scientific knowledge available, even if coming from non-Christians. Given that healing was such a prominent Christian calling, eventually medicine became one of the highest fields of study at the medieval university. Medicine advanced there as human dissections took place and people started to question some of the practices of Galen and Hippocrates.[157] So medicine did advance because of Christian practices after all. And even if ancient medical practices were not always the best, just being offered a place where rest, diet, and nursing were provided had salutary effects on the sick.[158]

Today, many hospitals bear the unmistakable mark of a Christian legacy in their names. Just think of Lutheran General, Saint Anthony's, Swedish Covenant, etc. Of course, one could argue that many of those names are just vestiges of a distant past. Yet even when a monstrous bureaucracy caused by regulation, insurance, pharmaceutical, and equipment providers has taken hold of many of these hospitals, there is a sense that these places still bear some unmistakable Christian marks. They are often places where care is seen as a service and not a commodity, where patients have intrinsic worth and are treated with human dignity, and where financial aid is provided for the poor.[159]

So how exactly is it that today the state and private companies think that they can divorce religious values from this field? No wonder why costs have been skyrocketing for decades now. I do not want to be misunderstood here. I am not advocating that the church suddenly take over the entire healthcare industry and welfare. That would be disastrous since currently the church doesn't have the necessary infrastructure and resources to take on this task. But that's a shame given that in the past it did. It has been centuries of retreat to the roles therapist and event planner that has reduced the church to its current state. I hope Christians here are prodded to think creatively about how we can gradually take on this important task once more.

POSSIBLE OBJECTIONS

It is here now that I must answer to potential theological objections to what I have laid out in this chapter. I suspect many Christians will object to the church being inordinately involved in earthly politics, which naturally entails economics. Some, after all, have grown quite comfortable with having separate jurisdictions or spheres of influence between the church, the state, the university, and the private company. Three passages in particular come to mind that seem to counter the earthiness of Jesus' and the church's ministry.

First, when Jesus was brought before Pilate in John's gospel, Jesus said to him, "My kingdom is not from this world. If my kingdom were from this world, my followers would be fighting to keep me from being handed over to the Jews" (John 18:36). At first glance, Jesus here seems to state plainly that his kingdom is in heaven. If his kingdom is not from this world, where else could it be but heaven? This passage seems to evidently justify the popular notion that the church's job is to save souls so they make it to heaven and thus whatever happens on this ball of dirt is not that consequential.

But if we read closely, Jesus states what he means when he says that his kingdom is not from this world. Jesus says that if his kingdom were of the world, people would fight back on his behalf. In other words, what Jesus is saying is that those who belong to his kingdom do not follow the ways of the world, which at that time consisted of either ruling with brute force or inciting violent revolutions. Yes, it could be the case that Jesus was simply pointing out that he is from heaven and therefore he simply doesn't belong here, but I don't think that was the emphasis Jesus was trying to make. Otherwise, how could Jesus' priestly prayer just in the previous chapter be explained in which he says of his disciples, "they do not belong to the world, just as I do not belong to the world . . . as you have sent me into the world, so I have sent them into the world" (John 17:16, 18)? Jesus' mission for the church is clearly not to simply save as many souls to make it to heaven, but to be sent into the world as witnesses of God's love. The church does this by being united as one and thereby displaying God's love (John 17.:23), which, as I already pointed out, involves economic commitment to one another. In all of Jesus' priestly prayer, there is no talk of escaping this ball of dirt we call Earth.

Another passage that opponents of church involvement in earthly politics might point out is the controversy over paying taxes. When Jesus was confronted by the Pharisees regarding whether or not one should pay taxes to the empire, Jesus replied by saying, "Render to Caesar the things that are Caesar's and to God the things that are God's" (Matt 22:21, ESV). One could see why many would read this as Jesus saying that God and Caesar have two separate spheres of influence. Jesus seems to split the concern of spiritual matters with the concern for political and economic matters, as though they were two separate spheres. Churches today mirror this behavior. They stick strictly to the things that are pertinent to the salvation of the soul, while leaving the rest to the state to deal with.

Once again, Luther's two kingdoms doctrine comes to mind here. Recall from chapter 2 that the passage that Luther had used to support his position was Romans 13, which says that we must be subject to the governing authorities as they were established by God to yield the sword and to execute God's wrath on the wrongdoer. Luther's two kingdoms seems like a reasonable doctrine, for the church cannot yield the sword. So who else will establish order and justice on Earth but the state? It would seem then that Romans 13 seems to have undivided agreement with Jesus' words to give to Caesar what is his.

But like I've said before, it is just plain hypocritical to simply be peaceful at church and then wash our hands of all the violence incurred by the state we supported. In a democracy where those in power are Christians, Romans 13 and the two kingdoms theory simply cannot be used as a cop-out from the state's bloody hands. Here, context matters when interpreting Scripture. Hauerwas has observed that Romans 13 should never be read separately from Romans 12, which says, "Bless those who persecute you; bless and do not curse them" (v. 14).[160] In other words, the historical context in which Romans 13 was written was that of a church persecuted by the Roman state, not one in which Christians enjoyed power and prestige protected by their state. Romans 13 was clearly not written for Christians to get too cozy with the state.

As for giving to Caesar his due, it is good practice to first read the text plainly for what it says before providing fanciful interpretations. It could be argued that Jesus was simply talking about taxes, not whether the church and the state have two distinct jurisdictions. The material reality of the Jews at that time is that they had to pay taxes to the Romans and also to the temple authorities. Jesus was merely saying, "Pay your taxes, both to the Romans and to the temple," which would be no different from our situation today if we view the church as a colony within the state. We have to pay our taxes to the IRS and our tithes to the church. But some would still object and say that the fact that Jesus affirmed our duty to pay our taxes to Caesar goes to show that Jesus approved of the state as a necessary entity. Maybe. But it could simply show that Jesus did not approve of violent revolutions, and to not pay taxes to the state would have certainly incited one.

Yoder also observes that the very fact that this question was brought before Jesus goes to show that the demands and prerogatives of God's kingdom and Caesar's often overlap as they share the same arena.[161] If Jesus had taught that his was only a heavenly kingdom, why would people bring up this question to him? It is precisely because he taught that the kingdom is near that the question could arise. Moreover, even if we accept that Jesus is disentangling the jurisdictions between church and state, Jesus never specified the percentage of what is owed to the temple and to Caesar. Why are we to assume that the state should manage, say, 80 percent of what constitutes our lives, while the church only gets the remaining 20? Why can't it be the other way around? Shouldn't the latter be the case for those of us who claim to be Christians, a people that put God and God's church above else? Nor did Jesus here specify what roles belong to the state and to the church. Once again, why do we assume that it belongs to the state to manage political and economic matters, while it belongs to the church to manage the scraps of our inner emotions?

There is one last scriptural passage I want to address that seems to say that the church should not involve itself in worldly economic matters. This is none other than the story of the cleansing of the temple. In Jesus' time, there was much selling of sacrificial animals and exchanging of money on the temple grounds. When Jesus walked into the temple, he was so upset at what he saw that he overturned the tables of the money changers, drove out all the merchants, and then said, "Is it not written, 'My house shall be called a house of prayer for all the nations'? But you have made it a den of robbers" (Mark 11:17).

It is easy to get confused as to what exactly Jesus was upset about here. One might judge the temple authorities for corruption, as they surely must have been making quite a profit from this racketeering. On the other hand though, they were providing a valuable service to the faithful, as many had to trek tens if not hundreds of miles for their Passover pilgrimage. Every pilgrim was to bring an animal without defect to be sacrificed at the temple. Imagine what it would be like to travel with a sheep for days, making sure it would not get sick, let alone die, on the way. The temple authorities made the sacrifice convenient for pilgrims as all they needed to do is bring money and then buy the animals on the temple grounds. Why would Jesus disapprove of this system? Unless of course he was only upset at the profits of the religious leaders. On the surface then, this story seems to point out that the temple (or the church) should not get its hands on worldly economic activities. Involvement in these acts only ends up soiling one's hands and heart, as money is just plain dirty. And Jesus did say that one cannot serve both God and money (Matt 6:24).

But Richard Hays has a different take on what made Jesus so upset. When Jesus said what he said at the temple he was quoting Isaiah 56, whose context reads:

> These [foreigners] I will bring to my holy mountain,
> And make them joyful in my house of prayer;
> Their burnt offerings and sacrifices will be accepted on my altar;

> *For my house shall be called a house prayer for all nations.*
> Thus says the Lord God,
> Who gathers the outcasts of Israel,
> I will gather others to them
> besides those already gathered. (Isa 56:6–8)[162]

Isaiah was envisioning that all peoples, including non-Jewish foreigners, will one day be gathered at the temple and their prayers will be accepted. It so happened that the temple authorities had set up shop for their selling and buying of animals at the court of the Gentiles, the only place of the temple where non-Jews were allowed to approach and worship.[163] In their callous bigotry, the religious leaders simply did not care about Gentile worshippers, so they felt no qualms in filling up the space for the foreigners to their own profit. Because Jesus quoted Isaiah, it seems that this neglect of the universality and hospitality of the temple is what really ticked off Jesus, not that the temple was involved in economic matters.

The second part of Jesus' saying is that the religious leaders have made the temple into a "den of robbers." This explains the common assumption that the temple authorities were profiting from their temple shop. It may be true that they did and it goes to show that it is inexcusable for any religious leader today to pocket any money from the treasury of the church. We should thus be weary of following pastors who display a lavish lifestyle. But at its heart, Jesus' saying is once again a quotation, this time from Jeremiah 7, which is a tirade against those who had a false confidence in the temple and thought no harm would befall them because of it. Yet all the while they stole, murdered, and committed adultery. Jeremiah then predicted the temple's destruction, which took place when the Babylonians attacked (Jer 7:4–14). So when Jesus quoted Jeremiah, he was not only condemning the racketeering, but he was in fact foreshadowing the temple's destruction once again, as he did so explicitly later in Mark 13.[164] And we know for a fact that the temple was destroyed again by the Romans in 70 AD.

So it seems that the argument that the church should not be involved in economic matters does not hold after all. If Jesus was really against the temple providing an economic service, why did he feed the five thousand? Wasn't that a valuable material service to the poor and the hungry? As for the saying that one cannot serve two masters at the same time, it is precisely for that reason that the church should be involved in our economic lives. It is when we separate the two that we have made for ourselves two masters. When we have no clue how our money relates to our faith and still spend hours making and spending money, it becomes all the more likely that we serve mammon.

Throughout this chapter, I have traced the history of ancient Israel, Jesus, and the church to demonstrate that the church and its predecessors were clearly a politics that thoroughly integrated every aspect of their members' lives. This stands in stark contrast to the fractured nature of our lives today. I will attempt to provide some tangible solutions in the next chapter.

5.

Where to Go from Here

Possible Solutions

It is here that the ranting must come to an end (sort of) and concrete solutions be provided. There are myriads of books that point out the numerous problems of the church but offer no concrete solutions. Part of the problem is that books are often written by scholars in the ivory towers of universities and seminaries. Due to the fragmentation and specialization of knowledge as covered in chapter 3, scholars often do not know how the real world actually works. But I am not a scholar, at least not by profession, and my current job involves some pretty tough and dirty work in some respects. So I hope this work is not merely one more book that offers no solutions.

Like I said in the introduction, to really resolve the challenges before us will be no easy task. It will require a lot more than restructuring the one hour of worship service of a church or adding more programs to it. The only way to resolve the issue is by thoroughly reimagining and reorganizing the structures of our society. This will no doubt take lots of time and will require Christians of all stripes to pull their resources together, whether it be skills, experience, thought, or just plain money.

In this chapter, I will first offer three concrete examples from which I think the church can learn. It's sad to say that none of these are churches.

Two of these cases are not even Christian. I am sure that there must be some churches out there that exemplify a good politic. Yet the fact that the cases I draw from are not churches goes to show how far the church has drifted from the politics it used to be, to the extent that other organizations exemplify a politics better. Because these illustrations are not churches, I will not advocate the church imitating exactly what they do. So as I portray the relevant parts of each organization, I will also try to piece the parts together and pin down more concretely what I think the church could learn and do, not as a copycat, but on its own terms.

EXHIBIT A: CHICAGO HOPE ACADEMY

Chicago Hope Academy is a non-denominational Christian high school where I happen to work as a Bible instructor and robotics mentor. I am sure that there are numerous other schools out there that could just as much serve as an illustration as to how an academic institution exemplifies a politics. But there is something rather special about Hope. First, what sets it apart from most other Christian schools in America is that it primarily serves low-income minority families in the inner city. It's not that other Christian schools are by nature elitist or racist (though some of them certainly are), but the vast majority of Christian schools are constrained by the economics of a private school. Since most religious schools cannot receive funding from the state, they are forced to recoup from tuition their operating costs and the capital for future expenses. This means that tuition at a Christian high school in any major city ends up running anywhere between $10,000 to $30,000 annually. For a few schools, it's even more than that. As it turns out, the vast majority of families that can afford this cost happen to fall in the upper middle classes or higher, most of whose families happen to be White. In order to diversify their populations, many Christian schools offer scholarships. But the recipients of these tend to be a small minority.

But Hope currently has quite a diverse population of students, having a majority of African-Americans and Latino/as. How could this be? A little bit of the history of the school is in order here. The school was founded in 2004 by Bob and Tina Muzikowski, a wealthy couple that formerly worked in the insurance industry and Wall Street. They moved to Chicago from New York in 1988 and initially lived south of North Avenue, close to the prestigious Gold Coast neighborhood and just as close to the then infamous Cabrini-Green housing projects, which were ridden with crime. Though they worked downtown, as Christians, the Muzikowskis wanted to be good neighbors and initially partnered with Al Carter and started coaching baseball to Cabrini-Green kids. The Muzikowskis got an army of volunteers from their downtown contacts and friends to clean up a much neglected ball park in the neighborhood. Then kids showed up to play and the Near North Little League was formed. That a bunch of White business executives from downtown were volunteering and coaching Black kids in rough neighborhoods garnered the media's attention for a bit. Eventually an assistant coach wrote a book on it, which was made into the Hollywood film *Hardball,* where Keanu Reeves plays Bob Muzikowski. Yet the film producers distorted the story by taking out much of the Christian motivations behind all the coaching. The producers never talked to Bob or Al, and not a penny from the movie was given to the Little League or their cause. Later, Bob wrote *Safe at Home* to set the record straight, where much of the couple's Little League adventures are chronicled.

The Muzikowskis eventually moved to the West Side of Chicago, which is still somewhat infamous for crime, and started the Near West Little League in similar fashion. Much like people in the New Monasticism movement today, they were intentional Christians who did not run away from problems but lived right in their midst. That wasn't always very pleasant and sometimes put their family in harm's way. Sometimes they would lose Little League kids to gun violence. On one occasion, Tina was almost assaulted by a stranger who managed to sneak into her garage. Yet they did not pack up and leave, but pressed on. After years of coaching kids from rough neighborhoods, they realized that the kids needed a lot more than an after-school program that keeps them out of trouble, and so it is that the Muzikowskis started Chicago Hope Academy, also on the West Side.

The Muzikowskis dropped millions of dollars to buy and renovate the school's building and they even mortgaged their home. They also got some of the same downtown friends and contacts to continuously donate money for the school. Over the years, in order to make the school more sustainable, the school made good use of Bob's business acumen and started its own business called Chicago Hope Homes. At its inception, Hope Homes received donations of foreclosed and neglected properties nobody wanted from banks. Hope Homes would then rehab the properties and sell them for a profit for the school. In the process, the hope was also that it would contribute in rejuvenating blighted city blocks, which are vast in Chicago's South and West Sides. Now Hope Homes is a full-fledged business with all types of real estate operations. The school also owns a small coffee shop called Hope Café. The school's operating cost is paid by about one third originating from tuition, another third from generous donations, and another third from business revenues. The vast majority of students receive need-based financial aid. This is how the school manages to keep its population racially and socioeconomically diverse.

At its start, the school was not always so diverse. The vast majority of kids were Black kids from rough neighborhoods. But Bob likes to say that in order to improve education, you have to put your own kids in it. So it is that all seven of the Muzikowski kids have attended the school. The older Muzikowski kids were basically the only White kids in the school at the time. I do not know exactly how this unconventional upbringing has affected them, whether positively or negatively. But most of the now grown Muzikowski kids do not seem to regret their experiences. It rather seems to have made them more resilient and at the same time more empathetic human beings. One of them, Isaiah (Ike), came back to work for the school and poured out hours mentoring several kids. He started off as admissions counselor and is now the Dean of Academic Affairs.

Because the example was set by the founders, more and more healthy two-parent households eventually started to join in and decided to take a risk with their kids by enrolling them in the school rather than fleeing to the suburbs. The more there were of them, the more followed, and I would say that a good portion of kids in the school now are from pretty normal healthy families. Most may not be wealthy but many do come from wholesome families. This is truly what it means to "be with the poor," which is what Christians are called to do, rather than just writing a check. Educational research has demonstrated that this diversity is crucial to improve the fate of so-called at-risk kids. Middle-class kids often have a more complex vocabulary and higher aspirations instilled by their parents than kids from lower-income families. When placed together in the same classroom, some of that motivation for learning is rubbed off on at-risk kids.[165] I could certainly testify to this from many years of teaching.

Policy makers often think that they can just fix something by throwing money at the problem, and that is what has often happened with public schools in the inner city. If we are honest, kids don't really need more palatial buildings or the latest gadgets. They just need good friends that provide good peer influence. But how to make privileged parents send their kids to school side by side with needier kids? How far can policy go on this one? This is just one more example of how the state is incapable of solving certain problem because it lacks the moral authority to do so. Under such type of polity, parents will do whatever they think will make their kids most successful. What perpetuates the disparity between the rich and poor is precisely that the rich are increasingly sheltering themselves in private enclaves. What is the real reason a parent would be willing to dole out $30,000 on tuition? After a certain point, teachers, books, and technology can only get so good, no matter how much money you throw at them. The real reason why anyone would pay that much is to make sure that one's kids end up socializing with other children from the right kind of breeding.

Some here would be quick to criticize the Muzikowskis and other Hope parents for putting their kids at risk. I will not lie. The dangers are real, as sometimes it is poor behavior that rubs the other way. One might wonder, what right do the parents have to put their children at risk? Let the adults put their own life in jeopardy if they so choose, but not that of their kids. There is certainly some truth to this statement. But overall this remark assumes a very Western individualistic perspective of what children are. Many Christians hold to this perspective and one's family often becomes the paramount excuse for not giving one's life to God and God's mission.

But the reality is that such a view of kids is not the Christian view of kids. Children are first and foremost God's, not ours. That is why God has the prerogative to ask Abraham to sacrifice his only beloved son Isaac (Gen 22). Those who baptize their children as infants should perhaps closely examine what the church is doing with their kids (or what it did already). Christian parents often are overcome with sentimentality and think that they are saving their kids early on when having them baptized. But we should remember that baptism is baptism unto death! (Rom 6:4). Hauerwas observes that baptism and Eucharist are "the essential rituals of our politics."[166] As such, they set the standard of how we must live our lives. What happens during baptism is that the child is given to the church and then the church gives back the child to the parents and holds them accountable to raise the child in a particular way. So in some ways raising every child, even one's own, is a form of adoption, for we are raising the church's children, not ours.[167] Thus we do not even have the liberty to raise them any way we want, and often what we want is for them to be happy, successful, or self-actualized. But this is not the case with baptism. We become conscripted by the church to raise the church's kids to take up their cross and follow Jesus.

The Muzikowskis did not have their children baptized as infants, but they certainly lived as though they did. Surprisingly, their kids seem to have turned out just fine, or even better than if they had had a conventional upbringing. One would worry about their education, the older ones in particular having attended a relatively rough school at the time. But they ended up graduating from DePaul, Columbia U. (two of them), Wheaton, Brown, and Notre Dame. And because of their upbringing, most of them are empathetic enough to still want to support the school in some manner. Jesus' words come to mind here that say, "Whoever seeks to preserve his life will lose it, but whoever loses his life will keep it" (Luke 17:33). That's the irony of living as a Christian.

Going back to the school's story, I would like to point out in what other ways it lives out a politics, sadly more so than many churches. Of course, you can truly have an impact in forming kids when they are with you for an entire week rather than for only about an hour during Sunday school. Yes, it's that, but also at a most basic level the school at least provides a tangible service to the community, which in turn has wide-ranging economic repercussions in the long run. Sure, there are some kids who enjoy some of the learning for its own sake, but everyone comes here ultimately to get a degree. Their diploma then provides them with the opportunity to pursue a bachelor's degree elsewhere. This is no small feat as many of our graduates have been the first in their family to attend college. Once they do this, they become more financially independent, come back and help their families, or at the very least set a good example for them. The point is that the school provides an economic and educational service, distributing this good to those in need in similar fashion as the early church. Those who can afford the full tuition pay it, while those who cannot are given financial assistance.

Having a tangible good at stake makes a world of difference on other aspects of the school. The most important one is perhaps the area of discipline. Some have observed that the school's culture is rather strict while others that it's somewhat lenient on some kids. I think this seeming discrepancy is partly the result of the school trying to discipline students with law and grace at the same time, which is a rather difficult task. Overall though, our Dean of Student Development, Antwon Johnson, does a phenomenal job. Antwon is a Black man over 6'8" tall whose presence initially terrifies the freshman. Yet, he has been at Hope for over a decade and many graduates come back to visit him with a sense of gratitude (him of all people!).

Part of it is that he is the head basketball coach too, and people that get to know him closely realize he deeply cares. Discipline is dirty work and there have been numerous times in which the school has had to part ways with students. Yet what is unconventional about Hope is that in some cases those same expelled students have been accepted back a year or two later, after their case has been reviewed. They often return after it dawns on them that they actually had it quite good at Hope and are ready to amend their ways. Matthew 18 should come to mind once again. Recall that the last recourse that the church has in disciplining is to expel the sinner out. Yet the last step does not mean that the sinner is condemned to hell. It is rather done in the hope that the sinner will at some point realize his or her wrong and then come home. This principle is what is practiced at Hope. Overall, though imperfectly, discipline works at Hope because there is a tangible good at stake in graduating or getting kicked out.

How does this compare to many a church today? I've already pointed out that many churches are not in a position to discipline their members because churches often compete for membership. People have the attitude that they can simply join another congregation or quit church altogether, precisely because there is hardly anything at stake at the church. After all if the church has been reduced to a place providing friendships and therapy, what of those who feel they already have those goods? The reality is that they simply will not be receptive to correction. And so people go to church and often hear what they want to hear and do what they want to do, instead of being formed by the virtues of discipleship.

As I already mentioned, another unique aspect of Hope is that it runs a couple of businesses for sustainability's sake. Hope Homes is led by Kevin Drewyer and Brian Noller, who happen to also be the rugby and track coach, respectively. As coaches they get to know and love the students firsthand. So when they are at work doing their real-estate stuff, they are not just crunching numbers to earn a buck. They know that every penny of profit will go directly to help the students they are coaching. Do they really need any extra motivation for their work? This is what integration of faith with other industries should look like. When your boss is the kids that you are helping, you certainly would feel that your work is a lot more valuable than if you were a cog of a monstrous money-making machine. And why should any meaningful work be limited to teaching, preaching, and singing? People of any industry should be able to contribute something of value. But alas, because many a church today lacks involvement in economic matters, they can only make meaningful participation of their members out of preaching, teaching, and singing.

I should mention that some of Hope's workers have actually become closer to God through their employment at Hope. For a few, Hope has even contributed in their coming out of a crisis of faith. We tend to think that Christian organizations should only hire people that are solid in their faith. But Hope goes to show the role of work in the spiritual and moral formation of those who partake of it.

Hope Homes also has a direct long-term impact on the students it serves. Recently, a Hope graduate bought a home through Hope Homes. His mortgage application would have most likely been rejected by a traditional bank. But now he lives in one floor and rents out most of the building, which in turn pays for his entire mortgage. His mortgage of course then pays for some of the current students' tuition. Another Hope graduate got his HVAC license and is often contracted by Hope Homes. A third graduate works in the school as an assistant coach. Of course, touching the lives of a handful of students doesn't seem like a lot, but it's a start. It's certainly better than graduating a bunch of kids and then having them fend for themselves out there in the cold real world.

The school also believes in the potential of students to not just become good employees for someone else someday, but also that they can start their own businesses. So it is that recently a new elective was offered that cultivates entrepreneurship. Currently led by Peter Dukes, the EYE course (Entrepreneurial Youth Experience) requires students to start a real business as their final project. Throughout the year, students make class visits to various companies in the area, some of which have gracious CEOs or other executives who take the time to speak to the kids and show them around. Many of these companies are tiny, but some are well established, such as Coyote Logistics. The class is eye opening for many students as they come to see the numerous industries and opportunities out there. Obviously, not all final projects students submit are stellar. But at the very least they learn to capitalize on the skills they already possess. One worked towards making a graphic design business and another opened up a piano tuning business. Why do we assume that entrepreneurship is exclusively for those with means? People of all walks of life have the ability to start a business, become independent, and build their community and their church.

A last clarification is needed here. I do not want to sound like I'm romanticizing Chicago Hope or any other similar organization. Hope is an imperfect institution with flawed people from top to bottom, myself included. In meddling its hands on many aspects of an inner city community, it faces and creates numerous challenges on a daily basis. I've seen teachers, staff, and heads of school leave at year end for various reasons. I myself have been tempted to throw in the towel numerous times. Yet I don't think any Christian can deny that there is good and necessary work being done by Hope. Sometimes the most important work is the most challenging, and mistakes get made in the process. Though I cannot affirm how many years I will continue to work for Hope, the words engraved in one of our athletic parks come to mind here: "Let us not become weary in doing good, for at the proper time we will reap a harvest if we do not give up" (Gal 6:9).

EXHIBIT B: YUNUS SOCIAL BUSINESSES

In many ways, conventional banks perpetuate the growing disparities in our world. Banks will often lend money only to those of means. They assume that poor people will not pay back their loans and are thus regarded as not credit-worthy. Banks will often look at your salary to gage your ability to pay back the loan or will expect some form of collateral in case you don't, such as your house. These rules are an impediment on those who often need the loans the most. In poor countries, banks are often located in large cities, where wealth is concentrated. The loaning of money exclusively among the rich perpetuates the gap between the rich and the poor. Money makes money after all.

The microcredit revolution stands in stark contrast to what conventional banks do. Muhammad Yunus is most known for being one of the pioneers of microcredit. For those not familiar with the term, it is the loaning of small amounts of money to poor people as an effective form of aid. A small loan for a poor family can make an enormous difference for their living standards. For instance, suppose that a loan of $100 is made to a poor family in a remote village. Let's say that the family buys a goat. They then bottle its milk and sell it to their neighbors. The income generated can help provide for school supplies for the children so that they are able to attend school. With this concept in mind and noticing that banks only lent to the rich, Yunus started Grameen Bank in Bangladesh in 1983. It mostly lent to poor women, who turned out to be quite credit-worthy. It empowered them by fostering entrepreneurship, thus lifting their families out of poverty.[168] Due to its success, microcredit spread to many other impoverished countries. It turned out to be a more effective tool in fighting poverty than simply doling out vast amounts of aid, which debilitated people into dependency.

Inspired by the success of microcredit and examining the needs of the poor in more detail, Yunus then started another financial service called Yunus Social Businesses. In *A World of Three Zeros*, Yunus defines a social business as "a nondividend company dedicated to solving human problems."[169] A good business, after all, should have the mission of providing a benefit to society, especially to those in need. Yunus Social Businesses is essentially a form of venture capital for the poor who want to become entrepreneurs. Unlike Grameen Bank, it provides small investment funds rather than loans. Investors in the program get their money back plus 20 percent, no more, which is not a bad return by most investment standards. Entrepreneurs are responsible for paying back whatever money they received, plus 20 percent, after which they can fully own their company. The 20 percent pays for training, consulting, and accounting services for new entrepreneurs.[170]

Yunus provides numerous successful cases of entrepreneurship funded by his organization. One of them is Golden Bees, headquartered in Kampala, Uganda. Agriculture is an important sector of Uganda's economy. Yet many farmers remain poor due to their inability to access national and international markets with their products. Golden Bees' mission is to bring beekeeping within reach to small farmers who want to generate extra income. It sells beekeeping goods and services, such as training in beekeeping techniques, and then it collects, processes and markets the products those farmers create. Such products include honey; beeswax, which is used in cosmetics; and propolis, which has medicinal uses. Golden Bees now has a network of over 1200 farmers and has even received orders for its products from companies in China, Japan, and Denmark. Through its activities, it has lifted up the lives of all farmers in its network.[171]

Yunus makes it clear though that this success should not be limited to developing nations. Wealthy nations have their share of poor people who are often marginalized by the financial system and thus have no chance of receiving a loan or investment by conventional means. With the help of some friends, Yunus launched Grameen America, Inc. in 2008. In order to receive a loan, members have to present a plausible business plan and commit to keeping their children in school as well as nurturing the health and well-being of their families. As of 2017, this organization has nineteen branches in twelve cities such as New York and Los Angeles. It helps mostly poor women, many of whom are undocumented immigrants and would otherwise not have access to financial services. Members have received more than $590 million and have maintained a repayment rate of over 99 percent.[172]

At the heart of what Yunus has accomplished is a new paradigm for envisioning the foundations of our economic system. Our current system is based on the assumption that human beings are selfish by nature and will act in order to maximize their personal benefit most of the time. It's almost as though "selfish" is the equivalent of "rational" for economists. But according to Yunus's observations, this image of the selfish capitalist man is far divorced from reality. A real person is indeed sometimes selfish, but is at the same time caring, trusting, and selfless on many occasions. Many a real person works not only to make money but to enhance society, to protect the environment and just to bring more joy, beauty, and love into the world. One only needs to look at the millions of people who choose to be schoolteachers, social workers, nurses, firefighters, and non-profit workers when they could have chosen a more lucrative profession. Even in the business world, relationships are often built on personal trust. Even people who have made billions have pledged to give most of it away. Most people that became rich did not become so because they were bad people.[173] Yet, how many economic metrics are designed to measure a human touch of altruism?

What would it look like to redesign at least part of the financial system so that it takes into account real people with complex motivations beyond just greed? Yunus does not believe that the solution lies simply in progressive taxation by the state to redistribute wealth.[174] Nor does he think that the solution lies in poor people simply having better access to jobs. Such solutions assume that the world players and its wealth are involved in a zero-sum game. The mentality of job seeking and job providing, no matter how highly paid those jobs may be, is ultimately one that creates dependency. Yet most of our educational system is built with the goal in mind of producing people that will successfully land a job. The economic metric of unemployment used by most governments also presumes that normalcy for most people is simply landing a job.[175]

But Yunus believes that people have an unlimited creative capacity that can manifest itself through entrepreneurship. If you don't have a job, make your own! Yunus's solution, then, is the creation of social businesses and the infrastructure needed to cultivate them. Providing that financial infrastructure is what Yunus Social Businesses has been about. The success of this economic model has garnered the attention of various universities worldwide, and some have established Yunus Social Business Centres to teach courses and do research and consulting work for potential social businesses.[176]

Here I would like to point out the extent to which Yunus's ideas are in line with the thesis of this book. We both believe that the solution does not lie primarily on the state providing jobs or redistributing wealth through taxation, though those things can help. Our clinging to the nation-state as the solution for all our problems blurs our economic vision. Yunus and I both believe that the primary solution lies outside of the state in the microeconomic spaces that communities and individuals can create. It has been my proposal that the church should carry on such a task as it once did in the past. Though Yunus is not a Christian, his observations on human nature are in line with that of the Christian faith. We Christians believe that we are made in God's image and therefore carry in us godly qualities such as goodness, hospitality, and creativity. Much of this can be manifested in the work that we do or the businesses we create. We were not created to become a bunch of selfish capitalist pigs. Yet I suspect that many Christians end up becoming so because often times the system only allows them to thrive as such. Much of the system is, after all, devoid of moral values. I am arguing in this book that it is up to us to change things systemically rather than simply seeking a better job if we don't like our current one. There is much to learn from Muhammed Yunus in pursuing this important task.

EXHIBIT C: ELON MUSK AND HIS COMPANIES

Lately, Elon Musk has deservedly received some pretty bad press. It has become evident that the CEO of the most successful electric car company often overpromises and underdelivers. That was certainly the case when Tesla had a hard time reaching his promised production goals for the latest Model 3. Musk called it "production hell" as it required that he live and sleep at the factory daily, addressing inefficiencies and bottlenecks. He spent his birthday alone doing so and he almost missed his brother's wedding. He choked up describing an excruciating year in an interview with *The New York Times*.[177] Though the interview may have elicited empathy from some, he didn't get any from investors, making the stock slide. Then the stock slid even more after he smoked pot in an interview with Joe Rogan.[178] Before the *Times* interview, he got into a spat with a scuba diver, Vern Unsworth, who heroically rescued some teens of a soccer team caught in a cave in Thailand. The diver had mocked Musk for sending a mini-submarine to rescue the boys as a PR stunt. Musk replied with a tweet that the diver was a "pedo," offering no evidence whatsoever.[179]

To make matters worse, also earlier, Musk had tweeted that he had "funding secure" to take the company private, making Tesla's stock soar, just to fall flat when it turned out that funding was not so secure. The Securities and Exchange Commission later investigated the incident and fined him $20 million plus an extra $20 million to the company for failing to reign in Musk's tweets. After the settlement took place, Musk tweeted again, mocking the SEC as "Shortseller Enrichment Commission."[180] It didn't help that many employees of Tesla, including those in executive positions, were leaving the company in droves since around 2017.[181] Some former employees reported that they were fired for trying to organize a union and that a culture of fear persists.[182] As for his personal life, Musk is twice divorced even though he has five kids. All of this bad press of late may make one think that the billionaire entrepreneur is your typical Silicon Valley douchebag. The union-busting story of Tesla may also give the impression that Musk is your typical capitalist CEO, abusive of power. I suppose that in many ways he has become one. So you may ask, why am I bothering to mention Musk as an example in this book? Doesn't he represent much of what I'm arguing against here?

Yet, those who are geeky enough like me to have followed Musk's career closely know that this is an incomplete picture of his persona. Elon Musk is no doubt an extraordinary human being and a hundred years from now will be remembered as more than the Thomas Edison of the twenty-first century. He is not only the founder and CEO of Tesla. He also started PayPal, SpaceX, the Boring Company, Neuralink, OpenAI, and helped with the start and acquisition of SolarCity. Many of these corporations have served the greater good and have employed tens of thousands of workers. It is simply astonishing than an individual's accomplishments surpassed what any powerful nation-state could do on many areas. If anything, Elon shatters our perception that only the nation-state is capable of accomplishing worthy goals at a grand scale. This captivity of our imagination that the state holds is what I'm trying to dispel here in telling Elon's story.

It is worth recounting Musk's story from his early years. Elon was born and grew up in South Africa. His maternal grandparents were originally from Canada but eventually settled in South Africa.[183] From a young age, Elon was a bookworm and he seemed to have a book in his hands at all times. In his brother Kimbal's memory, Elon could plow through two books in a day. He had a particular liking towards comic books, but he read everything a boy could find in a library, fiction or nonfiction, until he ran out of books to read. He even went through the *Encyclopedia Britannica* at his local library.[184] When his parent's got divorced, Elon decided to live with his father, simply because it seemed unfair that his mother would get all the kids.[185] That was a fateful decision because his father was an engineer who sometimes required his boys to visit his job sites. Elon and Kimbal learned early how to lay bricks, install plumbing, fit windows, and do electrical wiring.[186] At the age of ten, Elon spotted a computer in an electronics shop and hounded his father to get one for him. Now, instead of sinking his head in a book, he would do so on his newly found toy. He learned BASIC programming language in about three days without getting sleep.[187] At the age of twelve, Elon first became famous by publishing his first working program in a South African magazine for $500. It was a video game he named Blastar, in which players had to destroy an alien space freighter.[188]

Things were not so bright in Elon's childhood though. Not only was his father very tough on the boys, but also, because of his shy and nerdy character, Elon had a hard time fitting in at school and was the victim of vicious bullying. In eight grade, he and Kimbal were sitting atop a concrete flight of stairs when suddenly a handful of boys came and shoved him down the stairs. Then they kicked him on the side and bashed his head against the ground. Elon blacked out. With a face bloodied and swollen, he was hospitalized for a week. Apparently, it was all for accidentally bumping into a bully at assembly. The bullying and isolation was relentless and did not stop for three or four years. They even beat up some of his few friends so they wouldn't hang out with him.[189] I may seem to be digressing here, but I think telling this part of Musk's story is important. I think Elon has been a hope and inspiration to all the nerdy and shy kids out there, some who have also experienced bullying and isolation. He has done in real life more than any TV show or movie to change the perception of geekiness, to the point of even making it sexy. At the very least he goes to show that it's not always the jocks and the bullies who inherit the Earth. There are reasons besides money that Musk has celebrity status.

After graduating high school, Elon went to college in Canada and then transferred to U-Penn. After completing his degree, he enrolled for a graduate degree at Stanford but quit after just two days to pursue his entrepreneurial ambitions. In a beat up 1970s BMW, he and his brother went to Silicon Valley and rented a crummy office. To save on rent and to work all day, they lived at the office and showered at the YMCA. Their first company was an online listing of businesses called Zip2, not unlike the Yellow Pages, but on the Internet. Eventually, investors took notice and the company grew until finally Compaq bought it for $307 million in 1999, of which Elon took $22 million.[190] After that he went on to start his next Internet business, X.com, which eventually became PayPal. He threw $12 million of his personal wealth into the company, leaving him only with $4 million after taxes from his previous success. In 2002, the company was bought by eBay for $1.5 billion, out of which Elon came out with $180 million after taxes.[191]

At this point, any other person would just stash away their wealth and retire in comfort. But Musk was just getting started. His real ambition all along was to make human beings an interplanetary species that can assure their own survival in case something goes wrong on Earth.[192] Clearly, Musk is not a Christian and perhaps read too many comic books as a kid. Yet, his wanting to go to Mars doesn't mean that he has given up on Earth entirely, as too many Christians have done in their hopes of heaven. He is a man who has deeply cared about environmental issues dating back to his high school years.[193] It was with these two major goals in mind that he started SpaceX and Tesla.

Before SpaceX came to be, Musk was just finding ways to support existing research regarding Mars. Eventually he went to Russia to purchase some ICBM rockets to start his space exploration, but called off the deal realizing that he was getting ripped off. On the way back, he made a spreadsheet calculating the cost of materials needed to build a rocket and figured that it would be way cheaper to build it himself. He had no degree in rocket engineering but spent months reading and learning from textbooks.[194] And that's how SpaceX was born. Musk threw more than $100 million of his own money to start this company.[195] As for Tesla, it was not originally Musk's creation. A group of engineers from Stanford led by J. B. Straubel had an obsession for electric cars. They figured that lithium-ion battery technology had advanced far enough to give enough range to a car. They went around in vain looking for investors until they found Elon Musk. Since Musk had also been thinking of that subject for a long time, he put in a $6.5 million investment, becoming its largest shareholder. He continued pouring in tens of millions as Tesla made its prototype and eventually became chairman of the company.[196]

When one looks at how large both companies are today and the billions that Elon is worth, it is easy to forget the numerous challenges that both companies faced. There was a time that it seemed like both companies were not going to make it. The first couple of SpaceX rockets ended up crashing pretty early in their flight, while the third exploded midair, burning up pretty much all the $100 million Musk put in.[197] All the while, Tesla had a host of issues producing its first car. Each roadster was supposed to have a price tag of $85,000 but just the costs of producing each had escalated to $200,000, making the company unprofitable.[198] In addition, the then-popular British TV show *Top Gear* gave the car a terrible review, saying that its battery didn't hold enough juice.[199] And then came the recession, which meant no one was buying luxury cars. At some point the company was burning through $4 million a month with little to show for.[200] Musk himself had recently gone through his first divorce around that time. With all these issues at hand, Musk has reported that he came close to having a nervous breakdown.

At last, in September of 2008, SpaceX's fourth launch was a success. If it had failed, there would have been no money for another launch and the company would have folded.[201] On December 23, 2008, NASA provided a $1.6 billion contract for twelve flights to the Space Station, saving the company in effect.[202] Also at the penultimate hour, literally hours before Tesla would have gone bankrupt, the company was able to secure funding. Musk himself gave up almost all of his remaining wealth to save the company. The deal closed on Christmas Eve.[203] Musk has admitted that all of this seemed much like a Christmas gift. In two consecutive days, both of his companies were saved from bankruptcy. Musk himself would have lost practically all his fortune had those deals not gone through.

It was fateful that both companies survived because their extraordinary accomplishments to this day should not be missed. SpaceX's Falcon-1 was the first privately funded rocket to reach orbit. It was the first time a private company, without billions of dollars from state coffers, was able to do what only a few powerful nation-states had done before. SpaceX also pioneered rocket landing, which meant that rockets could now be reused, reducing costs substantially. It is estimated that a SpaceX launch costs about $62 million, while it would cost NASA or the competition about $500 million per launch.[204] Before SpaceX, it seemed like the American people had lost their taste for space exploration, given that there were a host of other more pressing problems. Now everyone seems excited about the possibility of sending people to Mars.

Of course this is an expensive and some may say a wasteful endeavor. How exactly would these travels be funded and who would pay for them? Yet, Musk understands the importance of financial sustainability and relentlessly innovates proposing new business ideas. In recent years, he suggested that rockets could be used for Earth-to-Earth transit, making a flight from New York to Paris in thirty minutes.[205] More recently, he has been working on a plan to create a network of satellites that can bring blazing-speed Internet to all parts of the globe, which some have argued would be highly profitable for the company.[206] There are obviously logistical issues to be overcome for such plans to work, but what they go to show is that even a space endeavor with expensive goals has options to sustain itself without having to rely directly on tax dollars. It really is remarkable that a group of committed people organized under the polity of a company can achieve a lot more with a lot less than the nation-state.

As for Tesla, the company has grown to the extent that as of October 2018, it surpassed Mercedes-Benz in total car sales in the US. Its Model 3 outsold all other midsize luxury sedans combined (Mercedes-Benz, Jaguar, BMW, Audi, Lexus).[207] The company is also producing a semitruck and a pickup truck, which have already garnered interest from big-box retailers. This makes Tesla a crucial player in the fight against climate change, given that transportation is the single largest greenhouse-gas-emitting sector.[208] That's not even counting the fact that Tesla is involved in other industries such as the production of solar roofs. Once again, it seems that a private company is doing more to curb greenhouse gases than the state!

In some respects, Tesla and SpaceX are like large "social businesses." They demonstrate that a social business does not have to be limited to small shops that help impoverished communities, much like Yunus describes. On paper, SpaceX and Tesla are not organized as social business, but think of the original intent of their founder. Were they started by Musk to make more money for himself? He certainly was not in need of any after coming out with $180 million from the sale of PayPal. Why else would he have sacrificed his fortune and arguably his marriage in order to save both companies when they were at the verge of bankruptcy? The only possible reason is that he passionately believed in the social good that his companies would bring to the world. Yunus was right in saying that not all businesses are motivated by greed. It's too bad that Musk is not a Christian. If only people were excited about church as much as every rocket launch at the SpaceX headquarters. But doers don't always get that excited about social events as much. I think there is much that the church could learn from Elon Musk here.

THE CHURCH AS POLIS: HAVING GOODS IN COMMON

I have so far reviewed three cases that are not the church, but that in some ways exemplify a better politics than many of our churches. All these cases are a politics in so far as they provide and distribute an economic and social good for those involved. Politics is ultimately tied to economics because it is about figuring out what goods we hold in common and how to distribute these goods. The cases reviewed so far offer the goods of education, jobs, sense of purpose, community, and real solutions to numerous problems in our world. Perhaps the above cases do not embody as big a politics as the nation-state, yet they illustrate that it is possible for a smaller politics not only to supplement what the state does but even to do things better, as Musk's case clearly illustrates. I am not arguing here that the church should imitate everything these organizations do, for they are ultimately not the church. In the following sections I will attempt to put all the pieces together—what the church used to be, combined with the above present cases—in order to provide real viable solutions that are appropriate for the church today.

If much of the problem is that the church has lost any relevant involvement in our economic life, how should it get back into the game? Is it enough for churches to just write more checks to their favorite charities? If the church is our true political body, then it should act like a true governing body and collect taxes in order to provide and distribute necessary goods and services to its members. The church already collects tithes, but like I've said, not many people pay a full tithe. And why should they, given that they don't get much back from the church except for social events and a little therapy? But if the church actually provided something tangible, then it could compel its members to pay their dues. Moreover, it could provide real discipline and shape its members according to the virtues. After all, for most people, only when they have something at stake can they be corrected.

What things then could the church provide? Many large churches already set aside a portion of their budget to support charitable organizations such as World Vision or Doctors Without Borders. Taking care of the neediest around the world is certainly the church's duty and the church should continue to do so. Yet, if only those who are poor in distant lands are helped, it creates a sense of otherness regarding the poor. But Christians are called to be with the poor and not just write checks to them. How then can one truly be in communion with the poor? Of course, Jesus has called us to give up our possessions and be with them. But I understand that most of us will not do this from one day to another. Perhaps a good start then would be to recognize in what ways we are all poor, and thus have something in common with the poorest, even those of us here in America. For this introspection to take place, the church must not only provide for those in need outside of its walls, but also within its walls. In a country that values self-sufficiency, we tend to think it humiliating to receive help. We tend to think that we must be givers, but we must also learn to acknowledge our poverty and humbly receive. Only then can we learn that we live truly in community, dependent on those around us, even those who sometimes annoy us.

What would this look like? I currently attend West Loop Church, a small church of about forty mostly middle-class members. Like every good church should, many are committed in serving those in need outside its walls. Thus a portion of the tithe is used to support ministries that help the homeless, such as those that provide food pantries. My wife and a number of church members have volunteered by serving food to the poor and having fellowship with them. Yet the church doesn't stop at just providing for the needy outside of its walls. When a fellow church member falls into hard times, the church makes sure it provides some form of financial help. If a close family member of a congregant dies, the church partially pays for funeral expenses. If someone has an accident, the church partially pays for hospital bills. If someone needs rehab from some addiction, the church pays. The church even paid for part of the tuition for a Master of Divinity for one of its members. You might wonder how such a small church manages to have enough on its budget for expenses like that. Let me address budget scarcity issues later, but I do think there are solutions for this issue too. In no way am I saying here that West Loop Church embodies a sufficient politics, for the above issues are rather small compared to the larger economy. But these examples provide at least a start to the conversation.

We must ask ourselves, perhaps counterintuitively, what are the things we can share in common, so we are more dependent on one another? This is, after all, what the early church did; they held everything they had in common. That's what it meant for them to be a politics distinct from the Roman world around them. And only when we start doing so can we become a true community that fights the American individualistic myth of self-sufficiency.

Some here may object at the suggestion that the church should offer tangible worldly benefits. Aren't we supposed to follow Jesus regardless of the benefits we may or may not receive? Shouldn't the church stick to strictly offering spiritual benefits only? Because if the church offered worldly goods, wouldn't there be a lot of people that come to church only to receive such benefits? Certainly that would be the case with many. But like I've said before, Jesus and the church did offer "worldly" goods in their ministry. They fed the hungry and healed the sick. Besides, the reality is that most of us are a selfish bunch, going to God to receive some form of reward, whether physical or spiritual. It may not be the best of intentions, but that's how a walk of faith starts for a good lot. It is in the same manner that the early church won vast numbers so quickly. Would the rapid growth of the church in the book of Acts be believable in any way if church members didn't take care of one another? The church grew exponentially because people had so many needs that were met by the church that the Roman world was unable and unwilling to provide. So they flocked to a politics that could provide their deepest needs. Much in the same way today, people from all over the world want to flock to the United States, the politics that seemingly provides peace and prosperity. In the same vein, people also flock to high-paying corporations and quality academic institutions. On the other hand, people are leaving the church in droves, the social club where there isn't much at stake. It's time for the church to reclaim its political role by having goods in common, even "worldly" physical goods. The next few sections provide specific areas where the church can more concretely have things in common.

HAVING EDUCATION IN COMMON

What would the church having a politics look like in something as essential as education? Churches should pull their resources together to once again provide a good Christian education to their children. Parents should have resources other than Sunday school classes from their church. How much are children absorbing for just one hour a week, where no grades or transcripts are given and therefore there isn't much at stake? Is one hour on

Sundays enough to overcome the influence of the world from the rest of the week in public schools? Surely this is an issue that most Christian parents care deeply about but find themselves with no choice but to send their kids to the local public school. All of this goes to show the crucial role Christian schools play in the life of the church.

To be fair, many denominations and the Catholic Church have already tackled this issue by having started schools affiliated with them. Yet many of these schools are affiliated to a denomination merely by name only, and perhaps a bit in their theological views, but not so economically. But I say, let the church offer significant tuition discounts to their members, proportionate to financial need. Some Catholic parishes do this already. Yet I think their discounts could be more significant to the poor within their congregations. This would be a start in having people see the church as a political body that collects taxes in tithes and provides tangible benefits. It could mirror how Chicago Hope Academy disburses financial aid. The church could progressively distribute an essential good, having people at the top pay more. The church would then not be so dependent on meager Sunday school classes to teach its children the Scriptures. It could also then discipline its members, given that now they would have something more tangible at stake.

I understand that this may not sound like a practical solution for many small churches. Starting a school is no small feat after all. But they don't always have to. If there already is a decent Christian school in the vicinity, a portion of a church's budget could be used for partially paying the tuition of needier church members for the existing school. It would certainly help many a Christian school to receive the patronage from churches in its vicinity. This would also make these private schools more inclusive and diverse. Why should Christian schools be for those who are mostly White and upper class?

To clarify, that I advocate the church paying for tuition does not mean that I oppose state involvement in education altogether. It would help if states allowed a school voucher system or something of its like. Many parents already pay thousands in property taxes and find themselves unable to justify paying extra for private school. The state of Illinois recently started a program in which donors can pay to private school scholarship funds and receive significant tax deductions. Many families now qualify to have about half of their tuition reduced through this program.[209] This is one of those instances in which the church and state could work together.

But I understand that the whole Christian school idea may not be practical in every location. Because we have let the state take over education for so long, there are many public schools out there that are excellent. It would be hard, let alone foolish, to try to surpass them by starting another school nearby. So it seems that starting or supporting a Christian school would work only in areas where there is a need, where public schools are subpar. Such was the case with Chicago Hope. Also, many Christian schools have sadly become a stronghold of fundamentalism. I get that they are not always the best options out there.

But like I said, we shouldn't just talk about elementary or secondary education here. In the past the church was at the forefront in research, science, and industry, often through the university. Why can't we do it now? It seems like most universities, even those that claim a Christian identity by name, have nothing to do with the church these days. But what if churches provided part of college tuition for members that choose to go to a Christian college? This would be no different than what the Dominicans were doing for their members. Moreover, this would provide a tangible benefit even for the wealthier congregants of a church so that they have something at stake in it. It would be an option for churches in wealthier neighborhoods that already have impeccable primary and secondary public schools. How many families can really dole out the full $200,000 college price tag after all? In America, it turns out that even the upper classes are people in need when it comes to higher education for their children. It turns out that it is also the wealthy that are perhaps most in need of discipleship, because people usually don't tell them what to do, church leaders included. Partially providing for college tuition would be a great way for even the wealthier families to have something at stake in the church, by which they would then become more accountable.

Moreover, if a significant portion of college students were at least partially supported by their churches, the church would once again have a collective voice on how colleges are run, what research they support and for what purpose. Many Christian parents quip that their children become quite liberal or lose their faith when they go out to the universities. Universities do lean generally to the left simply because they support novel research, and novelty is by nature usually more liberal than conservative. Not that students shouldn't learn to question what they grew up with. I myself went through a crisis of faith in college and came out stronger at the end. Fostering critical thinking is important, but at the same time the study of time-tested traditions should not be ignored. If Christians banded together through the church, their voice could be quite powerful at the university. It would take some time, but money does speak after all.

Is this meddling with the objectivity of research at the university? Like I've said in chapter 3, there is no such thing as a purely objective pursuit of knowledge. Corporations and governments have their agenda and they actively and constantly meddle in the allegedly objective universities. If such is the case, is not the church in a better position to give a moral compass to the pursuit of truth? And how could there not be an agenda for such an endeavor? I mean, should we just perform an aimless task that happens to be very expensive? It is a good thing that there will always be an agenda behind the pursuit of knowledge. Otherwise, why do it at all? And as I mentioned in chapter 4, our very notion of science and its study at the university arose from a worldview fostered by the church. It should not be so preposterous after all to think of universities at least partially backed by the church. And indeed it so happens that many of the greatest academic institutions are still religious in nature, such as Notre Dame University. Is their research compromised or stifled by a dogmatic church? Not really. And are not church-related institutions in a better position to integrate various areas of knowledge together?

Yet I suspect that many students in college often end up losing their faith more because of social environment than their actual academic studies. If financially supported by their church, perhaps at least some students would feel more compelled to live more responsibly instead of taking part of much of the debauchery that has become part of college life. Money does not only have the power to dictate research and teaching, but also what a scholarship recipient is to do with benefits. In some instances, depending on the amount of help given, churches could ask beneficiaries to work for the church for some time after graduation. Or at least they can set standards for what type of jobs or employers their beneficiaries are allowed to take employment with. Of course, each church could decide at their discretion which students would qualify for which colleges for such benefits.

In summary, it seems clear that in order to have better integration of the various fields of knowledge, a nobler agenda for its pursuit, a more altruistic application of it to industry and the economy, and at the same time a more rigorous discipleship of church members, including its wealthier congregants, more equitable access to quality education leading to better economic opportunities for the poor, then it is a no-brainer that the church should start trying some of the proposals I have highlighted in this section. If the church is our true polis and not the nation-state, then the church should take on such an important task and not simply relegate it to the state.

HAVING INDUSTRY AND JOBS IN COMMON

If the church is to reclaim any sense that it is a politics, it must once again be an economic body. Politics is about economics, after all. So how can the church reclaim its economic nature? How can the church facilitate or provide jobs besides that of preaching and leading worship that people would find meaningful and integrated with faith? If the church wants to stop losing its members to godless corporations that provide little to no moral formation, then I say let the church have its own venture capital arm. Does this sound outrageous, perhaps even immoral? But is it really? If one really thinks about it, how different is this to how the Augustinians funded enterprises and how the Cistercians became industrious? Also, if venture capital is seen as one way of investing one's assets, then think of the numerous academic and religious institutions that already invest their assets in various types of funds. Because financial managers diversify assets, surely some of those assets find their way into venture capital already. Just because something sounds like Wall Street lingo, it shouldn't be seen as this dark evil force. When institutions invest their assets, all they are doing is allocating their money into various existing fund alternatives.

What would it then look like for the church to have its own venture capital arm? To start with, there is a difference between a church investing in an external venture capital firm and owning its own such fund. In the first case, the external firm gets to make the bets and decide which startups or small businesses they will invest in. They will simply pick those startups that have the most chance of success regardless of the social impact they have. Any individual or organization that invests in such venture capital funds simply reaps a percentage of those profits. Could a lot of good be done if such investments are selective? Yes, but in a limited way. For instance, some funds only put their money in renewable energy companies. At first glance, it may seem like there are overwhelmingly numerous good choices to invest in. But really, how many of those funds invest in social or benefit corporations? Are there any ETFs or mutual funds that specialize in social businesses as the ones described by Yunus? Not to my knowledge.

On the other hand, a church-owned venture capital arm could lend a hand to members of its own community that want to start a business, much like Yunus Social Businesses. Yunus is right in saying that people should not simply be dependent on a job. If there are no jobs out there, let people create not one job but several by starting a business. As we are made in God's image, we all have a creative and artistic propensity, which can translate into entrepreneurship. Yunus also nailed it when he says that entrepreneurs are motivated by much more than money. A business has great potential of serving a social good. A church then could act much like Yunus Social Businesses and could loan or provide investments to members that have brilliant ideas for sustainable businesses and are also interested in the public good.

The benefits of such an arrangement? The church could provide mentorship along the way instead of leaving entrepreneurs to fend for themselves. Also, unlike traditional banks or venture capital firms, a church-owned fund need not base its decisions solely on the applicant's chance of success. A church would have the advantage of knowing its members and thus determine who are credit-worthy or could use a second chance, without having to solely rely on a credit score number on a piece of paper. It could also provide microloans or microinvestments to its neediest members, something that traditional banks simply don't do. The church could also choose to support only ventures that have a positive social impact in line with its theological views. These could be businesses that benefit local communities or have a positive impact on the environment. In return, the church could own a share of the newly minted businesses. Church members could also sit in the board of directors for each enterprise, making sure that it lives up to the highest goals and ethical standards.

As each business grows, the church could also ask that at least some of its hires come from within the same community. The church could make sure that at least a portion of those hired are among the neediest, such as people with disabilities or ex-convicts. Most people with disabilities are not disabled in their whole body and many ex-convicts have mended their ways, at least those that go to church. These groups are often fully capable to perform a job as good as or better than others, depending on what the job requires. Yet because of the stigma they face in society, they are often without an adequate job. But if the church is a true community that looks after its most vulnerable, then it would make sure not only that those in need have enough to get by, but also that everyone be a fully dignified contributing member of its body. The church often provides charity to the needy here and there, but if it is to be a truly inclusive body, it must also provide a way for people to contribute in meaningful ways to its life. How else to fulfill what Paul says about the church?:

> The eye cannot say to the hand, "I have no need of you," nor again the head to the feet, "I have no need of you." On the contrary, the members of the body that seem to be weaker are indispensable, and those members of the body that we think less honorable we clothe with greater honor. (1 Cor 12:21–23)

This scripture cannot be fulfilled by simply providing handouts to the poor or by inviting them to a social event, as many church events tend to be, but only by including all members as part of a community's economy.

If the church gets to own shares of each new business it supports, what would it do with the profits? Perhaps this is the part that may not sit well with some. Should the church generate profits? Does that sound too capitalistic or materialistic? Couldn't this lead to corruption? Aren't there pastors already who own Bentleys or fly private jets even without this type of arrangement? But it need not be that way. I already discussed in the previous chapter that there are enough theological reasons for the church to be involved in the economy. Sure, there will always be corruption here and there, but as long as churches are transparent and all members involved hold themselves accountable to each other and the church, such instances of corruption could be greatly diminished. The profits here should not go to fill the pockets of individual church leaders.

Where then would the profits go? Well, aren't there enough needs that every church has but not enough resources to go around? The church is supposed to feed the hungry and heal the sick, yet many churches don't even have the means to take care of their buildings. There are myriads of issues where the church could be more involved, such as stopping human trafficking and climate change, setting up more orphanages, clinics, schools, soup kitchens, sending out missionaries, etc. And as discussed in the previous two sections, part of a church's resources should go into taking care of the needs of its own members within its walls. Does the church not need profit? It could actually use quite a bit of it.

By linking new enterprises with the church, there are other deeply embedded societal problems that could be tackled other than just the scarcity of resources. I already mentioned that we inhabit a fractured world where we often don't know how our jobs are related to faith, family, politics, and other industries or fields of knowledge. Lots of people go to the grind from nine to five just to make a buck. But how different it would be if one worked for a company in which a church is a major shareholder? In this scenario, one would use one's skills not for the enrichment of a few executives at the top of a food chain, but for the betterment of refugees, orphans, the homeless, the sick, or whomever one's church is looking after. How would it change one's perspective to see such people as one's boss? This is what it would mean to truly serve Jesus as the boss of our lives, for Jesus says, "For I was hungry and you gave me food, I was thirsty and you gave me something to drink, I was a stranger and you welcomed me, I was naked and you gave me clothing, I was sick and you took care of me, I was in prison and you visited me" (Matt 25:35–36). One's workplace could once again become an exciting place full of meaning and purpose where true friendships are built. For true friendships are built when there is a common task to be done, not simply by watching a football game together. And if such workplaces were to be provided by the church, they would be a diverse workforce including peoples of all races, skills, socioeconomic backgrounds, people with disabilities, and even ex-convicts. What better way to make friends with these groups but to work alongside them for the common good? This is the way the church could provide true communion amongst different people, rather than just providing handouts or mingling events.

Many churches are located in rural or small towns that have been disenfranchised by an economy that favors big cities. Think of the benefits small towns could get if the church adopted this system. In the current system, a corporation is out there just to make a buck, so they do what is most beneficial for the pockets of its shareholders. Think of Amazon choosing New York and a suburb of DC for its second headquarters. They completely bypassed small-town America. As it is, large cities get wealthier while small towns are shrinking and aging. The constant disenfranchisement of small towns is partly what brought Trump to power. But if churches in small towns networked and started their own venture capital arms, they could require business owners to stay in their communities. Why should young people in rural areas have to choose between wallowing in despair or moving out to the larger cities where the jobs are? Couldn't they create jobs in their own hometown? If any such business grew and hired numbers of people, think about the enormous impact that would have on a small town.

This societal restructuring need not be limited to the church. Any nonprofit could benefit by following this model. Why should nonprofits be at the constant mercy of charitable donations, which often are at the whims of rich people? Nonprofits such as World Vision or Chicago Hope Academy could emulate this model. Hope already has the infrastructure in place so that this could happen organically. It already is the sole owner of a couple businesses, Chicago Hope Homes and Hope Café, which provide for a big portion of Hope's operating costs. The school is also connected to some deep-pocketed donors. In the near future, I don't see why some of them couldn't set up a venture capital arm so that Hope graduates that have a good business idea can come back and receive an investment sum. Donors themselves could make a profit from this while supporting a great cause. Besides, Hope already offers an entrepreneurship class and many graduates end up majoring in business and economics due to the influence of its business-minded founder. If successful, those businesses could provide extra revenue to the school and also hire future Hope graduates.

These social startups or small businesses need not be limited to small mom-and-pop shops that help local communities. Any startup has the potential to grow and become a major corporation that hires thousands of talented people. Elon Musk and his companies are proof that it's not only the greedy that end up building major corporations and brands. If a company provides great value for a much-needed good or service, then it can build a large customer base and make an enormous positive social impact. There are so many great startups out there that are already doing so. In today's connected world, people everywhere are becoming more creative and entrepreneurial and are embarking to solve many of the world's problems. For instance, some have managed to capture carbon from the air and make usable and marketable plastic from it.[210] Or there is the case of Boyan Slat, who founded a company at the age of eighteen to clean up the oceans by simply catching the plastic using the ocean currents.[211]

People out there are full of inventive ideas and it's just too bad that the church has been sitting on the sidelines, making little to no contribution to any of these exciting endeavors. Is it any wonder why many a millennial sees little need for the church? The only way the church can get its skin in the game and tap into the brilliant ideas of many of its members is to get its hands back into the economy. Imagine what the church could have been if the founders of all the above companies had come to the church for funding. The church should not just preach against environmental pollution, inequality, or human trafficking. It must practice what it preaches and actually do something! Yet because the church has fallen prey to individualism, all it encourages is for its individual members to do something out there. But where and how exactly are individuals going to get the resources? So as it turns out, many Christians just end up sitting on the sidelines or they leave the church for a politics that will actually bring to life their innovative ideas.

Though this is a pressing issue, I understand that starting a venture capital arm may sound unrealistic for many churches and nonprofits. Surely the megachurches have the deep pockets and the know-how to set up such funds, but what about the rest? Once again though, not every church has to do this on its own. Smaller churches could network among themselves and set up a common fund to which they could pitch in. A potential entrepreneur from any of the churches in the network could then present her business plan and apply for a loan or investment from that common fund. A portion of the board of directors of such companies could be on a rotation basis between member churches to make sure that not one church is benefitting in terms of the hires and decisions made by the company. Hard? Maybe. But certainly not impossible. For some networks, the feasibility of this could be dependent on some wealthy and generous individuals deciding that this is worth at least a starting support. These real "angel investors" could be entitled to a portion of shares of the newly minted businesses they put money on. It would also certainly help if church members in the financial industry volunteered their expertise, at least initially. If a task is so important, it certainly can and should be done despite its difficulties.

To recap, if the church is to be a politics, if it wants to provide quality jobs, true community among a diverse people, purpose and meaning in life through peoples' jobs, integrate one's work with faith, stem the exodus from the church, fight environmental pollution, disease, human trafficking, socioeconomic and racial inequality, provide peace and prosperity, or just do something about any darn problem afflicting the world, then the church must get its skin back in the economic game. I think that the above proposed solutions involving the church in venture capital are a way to move forward with this.

HAVING WELFARE AND HEALTHCARE IN COMMON

Welfare, which often involves healthcare, is also another essential good that the church pioneered but is now mostly controlled by the state and the private sector. Could the church take on this important task once again? I don't want to be misunderstood. I'm not here trying to provide a Republican argument for the abolition of state-funded welfare. Even if the church took on this task seriously, it would take decades to surpass the infrastructure that the state and private sector already have established to provide this necessary service. Perhaps the church never will surpass the state on this. Yet the church can become a necessary partner to the state. There are numerous religious nonprofits that are providing counseling, after-school programs, soup kitchens, and homeless shelters. Many of these organizations provide not only physical needs but also spiritual care, which the state would never be willing to do. The church must not only continuously support these organizations but increase its activities in these areas.

Though the state has much of the infrastructure in place, it is not always great at providing welfare, especially when it pertains to healthcare in America. The church should see such instances as opportunities to claim once more its original vocation. Healthcare is one of those goods that everyone needs, rich or poor. When sickness strikes, it becomes an acute reminder of our mortality and our need for dependence on those around us, regardless of our social class. Today within the church, medical care is often voluntarily provided by generous doctors and nurses. If someone gets sick in my church, one can freely ask our pastor for advice, who also happens to be a physician. Many Christian doctors and nurses also volunteer their time in far-flung places with scarce medical resources through organizations like Doctors Without Borders.

Yet I think the church could do more, a lot more. Healthcare used to be provided at some point almost exclusively by the church, but now the state and the private sector have taken over on the most part. Under the Obama administration, the state attempted to provide this essential service, but I think in many ways it failed to accomplish what it set out to do. Yes, millions of Americans became insured under Obamacare, yet the policy failed to lower healthcare costs, which ultimately is the largest barrier to receiving care. How beneficial was it for millions to be forced to buy insurance that had a $10,000 deductible? Overall, I think the failure of Obamacare was to focus first on who would pay for healthcare before thinking about how to lower overall costs. Its underlying assumption was of healthcare as a limited resource and therefore as part of a zero-sum game, so it turned out to be expensive regardless.

But if politics is about finding the goods that we have in common, then something like health "insurance" is where politics should be practiced down to the minute details. After all, insurance is about collecting people's money to a common pool and then distributing that money for various needs as they arise. Yet I'm not so sure that a profit-driven corporation or a supposedly morally neutral government can best decide what those needs are that warrant payment from the common pool. On the surface this doesn't look so complex. If one has contributed to the common pool, then one should get payment when facing an illness, plain and simple.

But it's not so simple when one takes a cursory look at medical ethics. For instance, what exactly is the nature and circumstances of an illness deserving treatment? What exactly constitutes good health or a good life well-lived? Should a private company or the state be entrusted with questions like these? To see what I mean, consider the following. Should insurance or Medicare be responsible for covering the costs for every Viagra prescription? To what extent is something like erectile dysfunction really a dysfunction? I would argue that it's a dysfunction when someone is in their thirties. But a dysfunction at the age of seventy? I don't want to sound like an ageist, but isn't someone that age way past his natural age for procreation? If we call it a dysfunction, it must be because of our culture's incessant obsession with sex. I wonder how women who were dumped at their old age for much younger women feel about the invention of Viagra. Of course, I use the Viagra example merely to illustrate that how we define an illness is deeply related to which political body we belong to and the values held by such politics. Viagra in itself is not that expensive and constitutes merely a fraction of our total healthcare cost.

But there are significantly larger expenses that are fully contingent to the values we hold. To put the matter into perspective, consider that medical costs are concentrated on a small segment of the population, specifically those who are chronically ill and those who are near the hour of death. Hundreds of billions of dollars are spent each year treating Americans who are in the last weeks or days of life.[212] It seems hard to estimate what percentage of total healthcare costs go towards end-of-life care, defined as treatment given in the last twelve months of someone's life. Reports differ in their estimates, but it seems to be somewhere between 8.5 and 13 percent.[213] Some see this is a modest cost, but "modest" is a relative term. One has to admit that it is still a rather big chunk of total costs.

Here, the term "care" is misleading. Hauerwas discerns that "cure, not care, has become medicine's primary purpose, [in which] physicians have become warriors engaged in combat with the ultimate adversary—death."[214] In *The Christian Art of Dying*, Allen Verhey traces this progressive medicalization of death in the modern world. In medieval times, a good death was considered one in which one's past had been confronted, one's sins repented, and one's peace made with family, friends, and community. As such, people strived to live according to the virtues even in their last hours. To die a sudden death was to be robbed of such an opportunity. But as medicinal advances took over, people have been trying to cheat death to the very last hour. How strange, for we know that death comes for us all. But in the process, patients die at hospitals with all kinds of contraptions attached to them, alienated from their own bodies, communities, and from God. The irony, according to Verhey, is that this "resistance to death . . . allows death a premature triumph."[215] I do not want to be misunderstood. I'm not advocating for eliminating end-of-life care altogether. But Christians should not be opposed to what some politicians ended up deriding as "death panels," which are simply honest end-of-life care conversations to be had with patients and family. Christians should also embrace the hospice movement, which in many cases provides a more humane and communal death, rather than one attached to all sorts of medical contraptions in the ICU.

Another huge healthcare expense associated with our values is defensive medicine. It's not just that the cost of malpractice insurance is high for doctors. It's that doctors will often overprescribe expensive tests and procedures just to be sure of their diagnoses and treatments in order to avoid litigation. Once again, the real costs of this is difficult to measure, as some tests or procedures are more directly related than others to defensive medicine. But in a study of three hospitals, doctors reported that as high as 28 percent of their orders were defensive, whether directly or indirectly.[216]

We Christians here should think about whether taking a doctor to court should really be part of what we do. Christians are supposed to be a people trained in the practice of forgiveness. It's stated in the Lord's Prayer, after all. Besides, Paul rebuked the Corinthian church because apparently some were taking to pagan court members within the congregation. It was so shameful that they couldn't resolve matters within the church and had to go to a pagan court that Paul says about the matter, "why not rather be wronged? Why not rather be defrauded?" (1 Cor 6:7). So why can't Christians make and have insurance that forfeits the right to sue a doctor for unintentional malpractice? That would make their insurance significantly cheaper. The only reasons to sue would be in cases of gross negligence or when someone's life is so affected that one cannot earn a living. America is a litigation-triggered country. People love to sue others for just about anything and attempt to make every possible penny even from accidents. This makes people defensive and unwilling to acknowledge mistakes. After all, admission of guilt is considered as evidence of guilt in a court of law. But that is so contrary to what should be Christian practices.

These are just a few examples of how "insurance" should be political to the details. Every community should be able to come up with what constitutes a well-lived and healthy life. And the Christian community's values should reflect a clear difference with that of the world. The problem is that private insurance corporations and Medicare will not think about such details. So the only choices offered are something in between catastrophic policies with deductible costs in the thousands of dollars to Cadillac policies with little to no coinsurance or deductible. And so it is that some will often end up footing the bill for things they don't always believe in, such as contraception or abortions.

I'm not an expert in the field. But given that such are the challenges, I am sure that if Christians have the will and huddle together, they can come up with creative solutions. There are already a few Christian healthcare sharing networks that work like insurance but are significantly cheaper. People in the program have to commit to a healthy lifestyle, such as regular exercise, healthy diet, or refraining from tobacco. This is a small example of communities with similar values coming together to limit costs. Part of the problem with these networks is that they are not for everyone, as some of them don't cover prescriptions or care for pre-existing conditions.[217]

Also, hospitals do not have to be bloated bureaucratic institutions. Christian Lawndale Center in Chicago offers quality comprehensive health care to the needy in Chicago. Of course they do this in partnership with the state, as most of their patients are Medicaid patients. Yet the fact that those limited payments cover most of their expenses goes to show that costs don't have to be exorbitant. Perhaps healthcare sharing networks should also look at the costs of each major hospital and determine which ones they'll pay for. A hospital does not need to look like a palace or a hotel, as many in America do. If these networks were large enough, that would provide incentive for providers to lower their costs.

Perhaps part of the problem is that employers are the ones choosing their employees' insurance. This means a few corporations, like Aetna or Blue Cross Blue Shield, hold something close to a monopoly on the insurance market. But employees should be able to choose to a degree what their benefits are and what they will pay for depending on the values of the communities to which they belong. There should be a push to weaken the stronghold that the few insurance companies have on the market. On this one, maybe government regulation is in order here.

Another factor that greatly adds to the costs of healthcare is the costs of new medications and medical treatments. The cost of some drugs is in the millions and their manufacturers face no competition for the duration of their patents. Big Pharma justifies its price tags by citing the high costs of research and development of their drugs. Perhaps the problem here is that we have allowed the bulk of research and development to fall on profit-seeking corporations. Were not the universities, which were at times founded by the church, the main centers of research? If there are any such things left as a genuinely Christian medical or pharmacy school, it should be their task to research those things that benefit society most. Professors in any field should not be allowed to simply research whatever they are most passionate about. They should not be allowed to specialize in obscure subjects to the point of absurdity. If they get paid a full-time salary, their institution should be able to dictate some of the research they do, so that it is for the public good. If any new treatments or medications should come out of such institutions, they should make little to no profit from such ventures. Of course, many institutions lack the equipment to carry out expensive research. Perhaps large churches with surpluses should provide the grants for some of these equipment. The church in the past was at the forefront of the advancement in scientific knowledge. It does not need to be any different today.

At the end of the day, if the American healthcare system will not get its act together, another possible supplemental solution could be to outsource large non-emergency procedures to other countries. America outsources almost all other goods and services, so why can't it do so for part of the sector that is truly breaking its bank? I know of many other countries that offer quality healthcare for one tenth of the costs.[218] We are talking about total costs of procedures from quality private hospitals overseas, without taking into account local government subsidies or insurance. So if a knee or hip replacement runs close to $100,000 in the U.S., one could easily end up paying close to $30,000 after paying the deductible and around 20 percent of costs. But if one pays $1,000 for a plane ticket and maybe $1,000 for hotels, one could still end up paying about $10,000 for the whole thing somewhere else, even without insurance. This is how those who know get it done, even getting a little tourism on the way.

So in extraneous circumstances, why couldn't the church pay for this kind of healthcare for its members, whether they have insurance or not? To be stuck with a $30,000 hardship would certainly affect a middle-class family, even with insurance. Why can't part of the church budget become a form of supplementary "insurance"? Once again, churches don't have to do this on their own. If the already-existing Christian healthcare sharing networks decided to cover their non-emergency procedures this way, they could substantially lower their membership costs. Currently those costs are cheaper than traditional insurance, but they are still very pricy simply because the cost of care in America is astronomically high. So it ends up being mostly the self-employed who benefit from those networks, given that those plans are among their cheaper options. If those networks lowered their costs by taking the overseas route I suggest here, churches could partially provide for membership costs to their uninsured members. Churches could be progressive in providing this benefit, paying for a higher percentage of costs towards their needier members.

There could be some other great ideas I haven't thought about. But I am sure that if Christians in the field got together and took on this task, then the church could once again be a politics that takes care of the sick.

SHOW ME THE MONEY!

I know that many are probably thinking that the church simply doesn't have money for this or any of the above daunting and seemingly outlandish proposals. Many small- and medium-size churches don't even have the budget to pay their pastor a proper salary and many a church building in the cities is in disrepair. So where on Earth are the resources going to come from for the above proposed solutions?

Yet if the church is to be a true politics once again, we simply cannot embrace the status quo. If we limit what the church can do because we can't see past the scarcity around, we are treating God and the resources God has given the church as a zero-sum game. God is the creator of the universe, the source of life and all that such life needs to thrive. God is not bound by our scarcity. To focus solely on our lack of resources arises from a Malthusian pessimism and a lack of creativity. Just take a look around and see the vast amounts of wealth. There are trillions of dollars in GDP produced in America alone, many of whose citizens are Christian. The problem, like I said, is that most of the activities that produce this wealth have little to no association with the church. Our task then is not to produce resources out of nowhere, but to restructure society in such a way that the church is once again at the center of life, which would then be reflected in the minting and distribution of resources.

It is here where I think it makes sense to have the church once again as provider and regulator of new industry among Christians. This is why having a venture capital arm is crucial. Not only does the grantor of a loan or investment have a say in the ethics and the hires of its beneficiary businesses, but it also gets to collect interest or a share of profits from them, sometimes on a continuous basis. Once some of its newly minted businesses take off, the problem of scarcity would vanish. Remember, some of these businesses have the potential of becoming large corporations, of which a network of churches could be shareholders. Imagine if a company like Tesla or SpaceX had received part of its initial funding from the church. We would have companies that not only have a meaningful mission, but behave a lot more ethically. And scarcity of resources in churches would not even be part of the conversation. SpaceX in particular should challenge the scraping-by mentality of churches and nonprofits. How is it that the most expensive and unprofitable of endeavors (sending humans to Mars) could manage to become not only sustainable, but highly profitable?

The real challenge then is to get this venture capital thing off the ground. After decades of the church sitting on the sidelines, there is a lack of infrastructure in place, so it makes it a challenge just to get started. Venture capital itself requires money, which the church seemingly does not have. To this challenge, I would say that the church needs to take a hard look at itself. First of all, does the church collect what it should in tithes and offerings? Second, are the church and its members using their resources wisely? Are there ways the church could cut on unnecessary expenses? And third, are there any wealthy Christians and people with the financial know-how out there, church members that could be convinced that this is a worthy endeavor worth investing and sacrificing for? Hopefully this book can convince at least some that it is.

ON DEATH AND TAXES

On the issue of tithes, only 10 to 25 percent of Christians are tithers, givers of 10 percent or more of their income. Christians are only giving at 2.5 percent per capita. If all believers were to give 10 percent, there would be an additional $165 billion for churches to use and distribute.[219] Maybe the church lacks resources because most of its members are not paying their dues. There are too many Christians who give whatever little they feel like giving and then go on believing that they are generous. So what makes Christians have such a lax attitude towards the tithe? There are numerous factors of course. For one, church leaders do not like to push their members away by continuously pressing on such an uncomfortable subject. The tithe seems to be slowly becoming one of those abandoned traditions of old. Many church members would rather give to other nonprofit organizations than the church. And who wouldn't feel this way, given that other organizations often accomplish a lot more than the church? Church leaders themselves sometimes even encourage this. Overall, the problem seems to be that people don't have a sense that the tithe, let alone giving anything, is a duty anymore. That's why they walk away feeling generous after giving a mere 2 percent.

It seems to me that the current state of affairs has come due to the loss of any sense that the church is a politics. But if the church is our true political body, then it has the right to collect taxes, which is exactly what the tithe is. This is why the prophet Malachi can say, "Will anyone rob God? Yet you are robbing me! But you say, "How are we robbing you?" In your tithes and offerings! You are cursed with a curse, for you are robbing me—the whole nation of you!" (Mal 3:8–9). The church is left dying because its members don't pay their dues. Yet today this Scripture would seem offensive to most so pastors do not often preach on it. In today's individualistic society where finances are considered personal, how can anyone demand that someone give part of their income? And yet we do give a substantial portion of our income to the IRS. If we failed to give our dues to the IRS, we would be put in jail for fraud, which is kind of robbing the government. So if the church is God's true politics, then when we fail to pay our dues we are indeed robbing God. Is there anyone out there that pays taxes because one feels like it and then believes one is generous after the fact? No. Everyone pays taxes out of obligation, not out of feeling. So it should be with the tithe. The two things we are not to be able to cheat are death and taxes. So how ingenious was it for Christians to have avoided the church tax? Meanwhile though, we are facing a spiritual death while we are okay with paying large amounts of taxes to the nation-state.

Some may quip that this is too much to pay. Why should anyone pay taxes to two or three different entities? In many parts of America, people are already paying income taxes to the federal government and the state government. And now they have to pay the church? Well, what exactly do we think it means when Jesus says, "Render to Caesar the things that are Caesar's, and to God the things that are God's" (Matt 22:21, ESV)? We already had a discussion on part of the deeper interpretation of this verse. But Jesus quite literally meant to pay both taxes—the Roman tax and the temple tax. Too much? Take that to Jesus. And that's the way it was in Roman times as well as throughout most of the Middle Ages. Is it more "enlightened" of us today to have reduced "oppressive" taxes to the extent that the church is left with scraps? And those who are left-leaning would not always agree that taxes are so oppressive. We know very well that taxes are necessary for the proper functioning of a polity. Fortunately, in America and some other democratic countries, people are allowed to deduct from their taxes a big portion of their contributions to religious organizations. This certainly alleviates the punch so that it is not exactly a double whammy on taxes. I'm sure the Romans didn't provide this benefit. So what are we whining about?

Of course the church does not and should not carry a stick to enforce this as the IRS does. The most it could do is to cut benefits from those that stop paying their dues. The problem is that the church today offers little to no tangible benefits. But if it offered benefits of education, welfare, healthcare, potential employment, or even investments, as described in the sections above, then it could use those as both carrot and stick to make sure people are paying their dues. But more than carrots or sticks, it is imperative that the church preach and teach on the political nature of the church. Congregants have to buy into this idea more than being coerced. This of course would require financial introspection on the part of a lot of families and individuals. They would have to cut down on some unnecessary expenses and learn to get by with a little less. But really, Americans are the most wasteful people on Earth. If they really analyzed their expenses, they could surely come up with places to cut down if the church is important to them. At the end of the day, it comes down to trusting that God will provide when we do the right thing. The passage in Malachi 3 continues by saying, "Bring the full tithe into the storehouse, so that there may be food in my house, and thus put me to the test, says the Lord of hosts; see if I will not open the windows of heaven for you and pour down for you an overflowing blessing" (Mal 3:10).

If this still leaves the church without enough resources, then frankly, the church has the authority to collect more than 10 percent. We already said that Jesus gave the church immense authority, to the extent that it can even adapt Jesus' words. Besides, people in the early church had everything in common, which meant that their taxes were not 10 but 100 percent. If that's too radical, there are proposals out there that fall somewhere in the middle. Ron Sider, who authored the famous book *Rich Christians in an Age of Hunger*, proposes what he calls a "graduated tithe," which is much like a progressive tax. He considers the base to be the U.S. poverty line, and anyone earning above it should pay more than 10 percent, incrementally.[220] If the IRS can collect more than 10 percent, why can't God and God's church, to whom everything belongs? Once again, are we Americans first or Christians first? But I understand that this may not sit well among many wealthy Christians. Perhaps asking people to give more than 10 percent should be limited to extraneous circumstances, like when the congregation faces an emergency. But at the end of the day, we must always remember that everything we have belongs to God and be ready to give up more than 10 percent when circumstances call for it. There is a lot of literature out there about how pastors can encourage their congregations to be more generous. But they are all missing the point. It's not about generosity but about obligation, plain and simple.

THE BUREAUCRATIC CHURCH

The second issue I mentioned was that some churches need to pare down their expenses. For a start, people should run away fast from congregations in which pastors drive luxurious cars and fly private jets. No matter how much money a church may have, it is inexcusable for any church leader to aggrandize their pockets from the Lord's money to live lavishly. But these churches aside, there are lots of other congregations who seem to barely pay their bills. This is no doubt the result of a shrinking church. As churches age and lose young professionals, they naturally have less people contributing to their coffers. Of course, some struggling churches will have to ask themselves whether their Gothic-like buildings are really worth maintaining. Some stained-glass windows can cost upwards of six-figure sums. Some other churches will have to ask themselves whether they spend too much on entertaining their crowds. Are those strobe lights really necessary for worship?

Yet I think that more than paring down single expenses here and there, ultimately we need to put into question the very expensive structures that have placed our church leaders in power. Perhaps some large denominations have become bloated bureaucracies over time. Many have established a system of ordination in which those who want to become leaders have to go to the seminaries that the church has established, which turns out to be a rather expensive endeavor. Meanwhile those seminaries operate much like modern universities and those that sit in its chairs have a rather nice gig. They have job security for simply reading and writing books about obscure and highly specialized subjects whose utility to the church is often dubious. Much like the university, seminary professors are often not heavily judged by their teaching but by their research. And for more than a century, biblical studies used to be all about historical and source criticism, pretty much taring the Bible apart for the sake of scholarship. What is a seminarian to make of all this? Some in the past came out of seminary losing their faith, and I still have seen this happen. It would not be surprising to find laypeople with more faith than their pastor. And then many church and seminary leaders fall into the trap of careerism, trying to make a reputable career out of their calling to serve. As it turns out, the church now has to reckon with what it has sowed, as it faces dwindling numbers not just in its pews but in seminary enrollments as well.

I do not want to be misunderstood. I do not want to seem like I'm deriding as useless some wonderful scholars in the seminaries. Theology is at the center of all life and practice of the church. It is therefore of upmost importance that the clergy be properly educated to lead the church. But I would question whether the current system is always conducive to this purpose. If the church is shrinking and so are its resources, it's time to put into question a system that raises career church leaders. Frankly, I've sensed an air of prideful arrogance even among some Christian scholars. Maybe they are far too removed from what happens on the ground, sitting comfortably in their ivory towers, which also prevents them from coming up with feasible solutions to problems on the frontlines. But aren't church leaders supposed to be sacrificial church servants?

I want to go back to the example of my current church, West Loop Church. I mentioned that it is mostly a middle-class small congregation that still manages to pay its bills and even pay for hardships that members go through. How can this church afford this in the city of Chicago? The answer is very simple. Our pastor, Ben Toh, does not take a penny in wages. Instead, he happens to be a physician who owns his own practice and therefore tithes substantial amounts to the church. Yet he and his wife live a rather humble lifestyle, more modest than people that make a lot less money than they. Does his training as a doctor mean that Ben does not have a sufficient theological training? Actually, he is semi-retired and has a lot of time to read various theology books and Bible commentaries. But couldn't he still benefit from a formal theological education? Anyone could, and I think Ben knows that, except for the fact that he will retire in a few years so he probably doesn't see much point.

One could argue that most people are not as fortunate as Pastor Ben and simply cannot afford to serve the church for free. This is certainly true. However, Ben was not always so fortunate himself. Before he was semi-retired, he was always so busy leading numerous Bible studies and tending to his patients. Of course, he wasn't a pastor then, but that doesn't diminish the work he did for the church back then. The truth is, he was not alone in doing this. Before starting West Loop Church, he was part of the larger University Bible Fellowship (UBF). This is an international organization with Presbyterian roots, originally founded in Korea in the 1960s, and has been up to now the second largest missionary-sending organization in Korea by numbers.[221] My father, who goes by his church-given name, Abraham Hwang, is one of those missionaries, still serving in Mexico. In the 60s and 70s, Korea was a gravely impoverished country, devastated by the Korean War. So one may wonder, how exactly did it manage to send so many missionaries? After all, missions cost money. The only way it was possible was by endorsing lay missions, sending out financially self-supporting missionaries.

What did this look like on the ground? Well, it was just plain brutal. Many missionaries had full-time jobs and then they were busy serving the ministry, which left them with little to no time to spend with their families. Like many others, my parents actually started their own business selling imported apparel and accessories, which made them even busier. With the money they earned they had to support the ministry and family in a poor country, which often meant there wasn't much for us. But like many Korean Christians of their generation, they believed in a theology of self-sacrifice, following the pattern of life set by Jesus Christ. UBF was certainly a radical and at times a controversial organization that has received some bad rep. Sociologist Rebecca Kim has given a more detailed account about it in her recent book, *The Spirit Moves West*. I'm not going to spend time here defending the organization, but for all its flaws I think it got a few things right. Having missionaries and pastors support themselves was modeled after St. Paul, who also did not take a salary and apparently supported himself by making tents (Acts 18:3; 1 Cor 9:14). In this way, though UBF was started in a poor country by poor people, it is today a financially robust organization.

There are clear disadvantages to this model. The most obvious one is the general lack of theological education among lay members, which was clearly manifest among some UBF leaders. If you are busy working a full-time job, how much time and money do you have to get a proper theological training? And certainly Jesus did allow those who work for the gospel to receive compensation by saying, "For the laborer deserves to be paid." (Luke 10:7). The church must also do what it can to attract its most talented into the vocation of teaching and preaching. This certainly does not mean that it should compete with Wall Street compensation but to make sure that a good pastor is at least provided for. In the past, the most educated were church leaders, whereas today they have gone to Wall Street or Silicon Valley. Is it any wonder that people would go in droves to hear someone like Steve Jobs give a talk while many church pews sit empty? Perhaps Paul was just a tad too radical in expecting anyone to follow his self-supporting example.

So how do we put these two seemingly contradictory propositions together, that of Jesus and Paul? Perhaps there needs to be a balance between both trajectories. Both extremes are not beneficial to the church overall. One extreme produces an expensive bureaucracy with career leaders who don't care much for personal sacrifice, while the other extreme produces theologically ill-prepared leaders. I do think that those who set the theological direction of a church or group of churches should receive a thorough theological training and should be supported with a salary. But does that mean that every single pastor and staff member has to get paid and receive a formal education? That would be nice, but that should be only to the extent that the church can afford it. Leaders ultimately have to serve the people, not the other way around. And just because one does not have a formal degree, it does not necessarily mean that one is ignorant. Like I've said, seminaries are expensive and sometimes not very effective at producing good leaders. It could work for the better if only those whose faithfulness has been tested in the church are sent to seminary, so that they can then come back and teach other leaders internally within the church without charging a fee.

Extraordinary times call for extraordinary measures. In an era when the church is aging and shrinking, the church has to learn to be leaner and nimbler once again. That may involve a painful introspection and eventual restructuring of positions, titles, and salaries. Contrary to the West, places where the church is growing rapidly are located in the Global South, a region that is significantly poorer than the West. Can they afford to pay their pastors in those regions the way they are paid in the West? Certainly not. In poorer regions, Christians just live sacrificial lives following the pattern of life set by Jesus. It's part of the spirit that Western Christians need to breathe once again. If we don't know how to sacrifice our time and wealth for the church, it must be due to the pervasive consumerism around us. But that's a topic I will leave for the last chapter.

Last but not least, the church throughout the ages has relied on an army of sacrificial volunteers to do all kinds of good work, from tending to the sick to managing church finances. It has also relied on generous donations of wealthy individuals. I refuse to believe that Christians today are so selfish that they will not volunteer any of their time and money. The problem seems to be that with the fracturing of various disciplines and industries, people have a hard time seeing how their particular gifts can build up the church. How exactly is a computer programmer supposed to be involved in the life of the church when the only jobs available are pretty much preaching and singing?

But if some of the solutions I've proposed above are implemented, the church will require and make use of all kinds of skills. First, it will require the know-how of those in the financial industry. Their skills can be applied for good so they won't need to be the pariah of our society the way tax collectors were in Jesus' time. Once venture capital arms have been set up, the need for other skills follows naturally. As people start using their God-given creativity to launch all kinds of social ventures, then programmers, designers, carpenters, and electricians all become quite useful.

When I think of the people of God volunteering their time and resources, Exodus comes to mind, when the people brought all kinds of materials and skills to build the tabernacle. God instructed Moses that "from all whose hearts prompt them to give you shall receive" (Exod 25:2). The work of God is not really one man's show, but the work of the people. I believe this is possible in our time again as long as people are given an adventurous purpose to go after. I hope that some of the proposals in this book are adventurous enough for people to pour in their money, time, and skills.

WHERE TO GO FROM HERE

CHRISTENDOM, AGAIN?

I suspect many will object to my solutions. To many, my proposals may sound like I'm bringing Christendom back from the dead. Carrots and sticks? Doesn't that sound like the church when it was in control, when it used to impose its ways through the Inquisition stick? And Christendom was not limited to the medieval church. When Christians were in power in America, there were places of power one could only get to as a Protestant White male. Is that what I'm trying to bring back?

I think we need to put things into perspective here. What I'm really proposing is not a coup in which Christians take power by force. That would be the only way a complete transformation of the economy is possible. Notice that I am endorsing neither capitalism nor socialism. Those two flawed systems could only be wrought by a powerful state that claims moral neutrality. Instead, I am arguing for churches big and small to stake their own microeconomic spaces within the larger economy, much in the same way private companies, nonprofits, and cooperatives do. As for carrots and sticks, any serious polity that claims to form the character of its members will have them. For instance, the smallest polity, which is the family, clearly has carrots and sticks to raise up its children. The early church also offered lots of carrots as they healed the sick and provided for their widows by having everything in common. But they also had the "stick" of excommunication, as Paul clearly commanded its use (1 Cor 5:13). The problem then with Christendom was not that it had carrots and sticks. Rather, it's the fact that its stick ultimately involved the use of the sword.

Only through getting its hands in the economy will the church once again recover a politics, form people of virtue, and actually get to accomplish something. The whole strife about faith and works that has sundered the church for the last five hundred years is really based on a false dichotomy. The belief that faith is all that matters could have only arisen from and be supported by a neutered church, a church domesticated by the state that doesn't get to do much. But James never saw the dichotomy and said, "So faith by itself, if it has not works, is dead" (Jas 2:17). Martin Luther didn't quite know what to make of the book of James. But if the church is our true politics, there is no dichotomy. The church, with faith, would naturally be doing the work of Jesus: healing the sick, mending the brokenhearted, providing for the hungry, and thus providing a true communion. It is thus imperative that we recover the political nature of the church so that once again we become a church of doers, not just believers.

BUT WHO TO VOTE FOR?

One last clarification may be needed here. So far I've expounded a lot on economic issues. The church staking out its own microeconomic space may sound really nice and all. But aren't there issues that the state, and only the state, can resolve? For instance, it seems like only the state has the power to curb abortion or pass a humane immigration reform. And these are some of the issues that many Christians get so worked up about in their support of the right or the left. So it would seem as though Christians cannot but continuously cling to one or the other political party to advance their cause. And so it seems then that there will be no end to the current divisiveness.

But I would argue that this line of thinking also arises from the captivity of our minds to the state. Yes, the state is here to stay and there are things that will have to be done in cooperation with it. But is government policy really the most impactful of things we can achieve regarding issues like abortion or immigration? The truth is that policy is drafted and signed within the halls of power at Capitol Hill or the stately desk of the Oval Office. Yes, policy does give directives, but at the end of the day, real impact happens through ordinary people doing the dirty work on the ground. Let the readers ask themselves what is more meaningful: a pro-life advocate protesting abortion policies at the steps of Capitol Hill, or a family adopting an orphan? The truth is, the church would be a great hypocrite if it only advocated for pro-life policies but then failed to provide for those unaborted children. Or consider, which one bears better witness to Christ: someone vehemently protesting Trump immigration policies or someone providing shelter and sanctuary to a refugee in their home? Adopting children, establishing foster homes, providing sanctuary and support systems to immigrants, are all the work of the church.

It's not that policy-making or protesting are unimportant. Certainly there is a place for those. At times, the church should make its case heard by the state, which can sometimes lead to cooperation between the two. But what seems problematic today is that Christians on the left and right fully invest almost all of their energy on making the state take action, as though that is the most impactful thing that could happen for their cause. Both sides attempt to make their case to the state so forcefully that I wonder if they have any energy left to actually do any of the work on the ground. Is this faithful witnessing to Christ and his church? When a position is advocated so forcefully that then it is heard by the state and forced upon its citizens, it just makes the losers resentful. According to Hauerwas, a democracy often is when "50.1 percent get to tell 49.9 percent what to do."[222] So it seems to me that those on the pro-life side often give the impression of being so completely insensitive towards the cause of women. Christians on the left and right have to remember that this is what happens when you win through government policy. On the abortion issue, of course, a baby's life is sacred, but the way that message is carried out has been through that of coercion through the state. And really, how many of those who are so passionate about this issue are willing to adopt a needy child? It's so much easier to protest, to vote, or to write policy than to raise a child.

The same could be said about the pro-immigration side. It's really easy to go out and protest or to write policy behind a desk, but how many of those protesters or policy-makers are willing to house and provide for a refugee in their home, or even just befriend one? I'm willing to bet that there are not that many. Some may object here, saying that immigrants are not as needy as babies. True. But do they really believe that immigrants, refugees or not, are in no need of some form of a support system, that if they just make it through the border through generous immigration policies they are going to be okay?

I am an immigrant myself and I cannot say just how wrong that view is. When I came to America, I wasn't particularly wealthy, but I was privileged compared to many other immigrants because I received a college education through a partial scholarship. But even still, during the early years I felt lonely and maladjusted, like I didn't belong. So I can't imagine what immigrants who come here with little to nothing go through. And I experienced all this while living in Chicago, a stronghold of liberalism filled with tolerant people. The problem with tolerance, a concept that liberals love, is that it ultimately means, "I tolerate your way of life even though I may not like it much. So you live your life and I'll live mine." No wonder why Chicago is one of the most segregated cities in the United States. But we immigrants did not just come here to make money, but to have ourselves and our children embraced by the wider community. It has become very apparent to me that welcoming immigrants and actually taking care of them is something that the church, and not the state, can and will do.

I do not want to seem like I am dissuading Christians from participating in peaceful protests, from drafting policy, and even from voting. These can all be very helpful. But no one should pat themselves on the back thinking they've done a great act of civic duty by just showing up to vote. At a time in which celebrities of all kinds are saying that there is no time more important to vote than now, I say that voting is one of the most trivial things you could possibly do to correct our situation. It simply does not compare to the amount of real work on the ground that needs to be done. I would go even further and say it would be best for some Christian leaders not to vote at all and publicly state so. To vote is to take a definitive side after all, and in some communities today that would create even more division along political lines. Does what I propose sound outrageous, irresponsible, and unpatriotic? Well, what's more important: to keep the unity of the church or to win on a few policy issues? Or does this sound "sectarian" to anyone? After all, that was one of the most significant critiques laid against Hauerwas. But let the reader judge whether any of the above proposed solutions seem like a retreat from the world. Let us remember then that it is the work of the church, and not the state, that matters most. So let us get to work on the things that the church, and only the whole church, can do.

Epilogue

The Politics of the Eucharist

The Lord Jesus on the night when he was betrayed took a loaf of bread, and when he had given thanks, he broke it and said, "This is my body that is for you. Do this in remembrance of me." In the same way he took the cup also, after supper, saying, "This cup is the new covenant in my blood. Do this, as often as you drink it, in remembrance of me." For as often as you eat this bread and drink the cup, you proclaim the Lord's death until he comes.

—1 Cor 11:23–26

I mentioned that Stanley Hauerwas once said that baptism and Eucharist "are the essential rituals of our politics."[223] It is in these rituals that we learn who we are and see the marks of God's kingdom in the world.[224] We may ask, how could Hauerwas put so much preeminence on the sacraments? I suspect that many simply see the sacraments as routine out of obedience to Jesus, who instituted the sacraments. But perhaps our failure to see their centrality is in part because many of our churches have distorted baptism and Eucharist in significant ways or they have been pushed to the fringes of what constitutes our worship. Some churches scarcely celebrate the Lord's Supper. But in the early church people assembled in order to break bread together, not so much to listen to a sermon or to sing a song. Those things were much later developments. The Eucharist was actually central to the life and politics of the early church. As such, I think the Eucharist brings together all the pieces I have laid out in regards to the politics of the church.

DO WE EAT AND DRINK IN AN UNWORTHY MANNER?

I suspect that during Communion many Christians go through the motions without thinking much about the meaning of what is going on. Yet Paul says that all who eat the bread and drink the cup in an unworthy manner, without discerning the body, are eating and drinking judgment upon themselves (1 Cor 11:27–29). Many churches therefore exhort their congregations to examine themselves before partaking of Communion. Because this is to be done in remembrance of Jesus, it is often believed that one should meditate about Jesus' sacrifice on the cross and to silently repent about one's personal sins before partaking of the Lord's Supper. There is certainly a lot of truth in this perception of the Eucharist. Jesus himself said when instituting the Lord's Supper, "this is my blood of the covenant, which is poured out for many for the forgiveness of sins" (Matt 26:28). The only problem with this practice is that it has often led to an individualized self-examination and repentance of one's sins before Communion. I suspect that even some Christians who participate in traditional liturgies may go through this individualized perception of Communion even if their church never meant to convey that message.

In some churches, particularly in the emerging ones, the Eucharist has been so deconstructed as to manifest and even encourage this rugged individualism. One church apparently has stations where one can choose to pray, or serve oneself or someone else Communion, or be served by a minister. A woman in that congregation confessed, "I really fell in love with the Communion time because everybody can respond to God in their own way."²²⁵ Still another church concluded Communion by featuring champagne and chocolate cake with an emphasis on being happy.²²⁶

What's going on here? Though many churches have good intentions, it seems as though the politics of the Lord's Supper have been so distorted as to follow America's individualistic mindset. It then becomes all about individual autonomy and happiness. Is it any wonder then that partaking in the Eucharist doesn't seem to transform the lives of Christians much? No wonder many Christians see the Lord's Supper as a peripheral rite of the worship service. And after the service is over, we go about our own individual lives. Like I said in my introduction, we go back to the seclusion and safety of our homes, some of which are significantly larger than others'. The following morning, some of us go to work for our government, most for a large corporation, while others don't have any work to go to. All the while we have no clue as to how our jobs bear any relationship with church. Then we come back together the following week for the same routine. Is there something amiss here? Are we not eating and drinking judgment upon ourselves?

COMMUNITY IN COMMUNION

Though it is good practice to examine oneself and repent of one's personal sins before partaking of Communion, the Eucharist was meant to be much more than that. In the First Letter to the Corinthians, Paul forcefully rebukes the Corinthian church for their many dissensions. When Paul addresses the Lord's Supper, he therefore says that those who bring judgment on themselves are those who partake "without discerning the body" (1 Cor 11:29). What did he mean by discerning the body? Was he really addressing the Reformation debate on transubstantiation, as to whether in the bread and the cup are the real presence of the body and blood of Christ? That would be anachronistic. Rather, the clue of what Paul meant is found immediately in the next chapter, as he talks about being *one* body with many members. In the one Spirit we were baptized into one body. The feet, hands, eyes, and ears are all indispensable members of the one body and should therefore treat each other with mutual love. He then explicitly states that the church is that one body by saying, "Now you are the body of Christ and individually members of it" (1 Cor 12:27). In other words, Communion is all about the church united as community, not individuals doing whatever they see fit. Hence the word *Communion*.

Now, was Paul just saying that the Corinthians should just get along during church and have nice feelings for each other? What specific dissensions in the Corinthian church was Paul trying to address? Though their specific conflicts were different from ours, they are still profoundly illuminating for our times. As it turns out, one of the many disagreements among them, as laid out in 1 Corinthians 8–10, was whether it was okay for Christians to eat meat sacrificed to idols. Corinth was a Roman colony in which it was common practice to have family gatherings or social occasions around sacrificing animals to pagan idols. Obviously Christian converts did not partake in the act itself of sacrificing to these idols. Yet some of the wealthier Christians may have felt that it was permissible to partake in the mingling or networking that such an event facilitated after the sacrifice, which entailed eating the meat that was sacrificed beforehand. It was simple social courtesy to do so. They argued this was okay because food is just food and idols are not real gods anyways (1 Cor 8:4, 8). Among poorer Corinthians, on the other hand, meat was not an ordinary part of their diet and some found it idolatrous that other Christians were eating of the meat sacrificed to idols. These poorer Corinthians may be the ones whom 1 Corinthians refers to as "the weak."[227]

Paul's answer to the Corinthians is instructive. He first acknowledges that the meat-eating Corinthians are right in saying that idols are not real and food is just food. This is the knowledge that they claimed to possess that puffed them up. But Paul then says that not everyone has this knowledge. Some Christians had been so accustomed to idolatry before that, their conscience being weak, they still saw eating this meat as partaking in idolatry. So if they see the "stronger" Christians eating the meat, might they not be encouraged to do the same, thereby sinning against their conscience? (1 Cor 8:7–13). The "stronger" Christians thought they had the freedom to eat according to their conscience, but Paul then makes it clear in the next chapter that it's not all about exercising our freedoms or rights for our individual benefit. Paul had the freedom to get married and the right to get paid as an apostle, yet he chose not to exercise these rights in order to serve people better. We Americans, who are so adamant about our rights, have much to learn here. Then Paul famously states, "So whether you eat or drink, or whatever you do, do everything for the glory of God" (1 Cor 10:31). Paul's view of the gospel is not that we are free to do whatever but that we must follow the self-sacrifice of Christ for the sake of others. In his commentary on First Corinthians, Richard Hays puts it this way: "Christ died for this person, and you can't even change your diet?"[228]

How could any of this apply to modern situations? When I teach this passage, I usually let students discuss and try to guess what the right position is on the issue without reading Paul's take on it first. I also provide more modern scenarios, such as whether it would be appropriate to have a drink in front of your alcoholic friend who is struggling to overcome addiction. The answer is clear on this one. One should not exercise one's freedom so as to not make someone weaker stumble. But then I also throw in a tougher question to my students, such as whether it is okay for a Christian to purchase a Rolls-Royce. This last question always leads to contentious debate, as many find it difficult to give up the individualist ways they have conformed to. Though the answer to the last question is a tough one, it should be clear from here that Communion is about being united as one body, not just about reflecting on our individual sins and Jesus' personal forgiveness.

CONSUMING THE BREAD VS. BEING CONSUMED BY OUR POSSESSIONS

In relation to the last example above, here is another issue that clearly caused tensions at the Communion table among the Corinthians. During Communion, apparently some went hungry while others had excess to the extent that they became drunk. In doing so, they were humiliating those who had nothing (1 Cor 11:21). This clearly goes to show that some of their conflicts were due to the socioeconomic disparities present in the Corinthian church. Almost immediately after addressing this issue, it is then that Paul talks about eating the bread and drinking the cup in an unworthy manner by failing to discern the body. Thus, "discerning the body" is about recognizing the unity that Christ has brought between rich and poor, servant and master. Given our growing socioeconomic disparities today, we must ask ourselves whether we in America continuously partake of the Eucharist in an unworthy manner. Going back to the opening paragraph of this book, if the Eucharist is central to the life of the church, are we really partaking in it the right way?

Of course part of the problem is our pervasive consumerism, which is a byproduct of our individualism. Here is the answer I give my students to the question regarding the Rolls-Royce. It is not okay for a Christian to live a lifestyle of gluttonous excess in comparison to one's community. I understand that "excess" may be a relative term to each local community. A lavish lifestyle in Mexico is clearly different than what goes by as excess in New York. But I think that a Rolls-Royce is clearly excessive by the standards of all communities.

What is the rationale for my answer? In the individualist mindset we live in, we think that finances are personal and that therefore the money I have is something I've earned, and thus I have the freedom to spend it in any way I want. But I don't think Paul would agree with that statement. Paul said that we are free, but we must use our freedom to glorify God by putting ourselves in the service of others. Can my freedom then to purchase a luxury good with my money harm others in the community around me? Absolutely. And it's not just because I could have used the money to give to some charity. I mean, why exactly is it that Americans have a pervasive problem of keeping up with the Joneses? Once you buy a luxury good, those around you want to keep up with you. You are making them fall into sin by breaking the Tenth Commandment, "Thou shall not covet." And why are Americans addicted to debt? In part because in their effort to keep up with the Joneses, many end up falling into the debt trap, which of course leads to a host of other social problems. Many a marriage ends because of broken finances. The leading cause of stress in relationships is finances, after all.[229] The rich could argue that those who are jealous are at fault. But really, is that what Paul was arguing all along? The "strong" should not use their freedom to make the "weak" fall.

So it's not Rolls-Royces only that are problematic. The purchase of any luxury good can become a stumbling block for others. Am I too radical in saying this? Consider this. How many teachers end up leaving their noble profession? I have witnessed countless teachers burn out and throw the towel because they felt they could not make it on their salary. I myself have toyed with the idea numerous times. Of course one could argue that the solution is simply to pay teachers more. That is most certainly correct! But frankly, another part of the problem is that some of us teachers simply cannot keep up with the lifestyle of everyone else! Is it not a stumbling block that because of one's consumerism someone else gave up a noble profession that serves God and others? The same applies to any other noble profession with a high attrition rate. Don't we make missionaries look stupid for giving up a comfortable lifestyle to serve others? If that's not a stumbling block, then I don't know what is.

I think it is clear that the Eucharist calls us all to examine our consumerism and individualism. This is one of those things that only the whole church can do. Individuals are powerless in the face of this monstrous way of life. We are all on this together, communal sinners that we are, for just as we have coveted, then we have acquired and made others covet. Only when the culture within the church is changed by the whole church, through the Eucharist, can people start living humbler lives. To be in community is to deny one's prerogatives in order to serve the other. Going back to the case of eating meat, Paul was basically asking: Jesus died for you, but you can't even deny yourself some meat? The same question today could be: Jesus died for you, but you can't even deny yourself that Gucci bag for the sake of your sister?

THE ECONOMICS OF THE EUCHARIST

Why was the Eucharist so central to the early church and what did it mean for them? Why did Jesus place so much importance on Communion by saying, "Do this in remembrance of me" (Luke 22:19)? To properly answer these questions, it would probably be best to start with the role that food has throughout the Bible, even before Communion was instituted. According to Lauren Winner, the Bible is "a culinary manual, concerned from start to finish about how to eat, what to eat, when to eat."[230] In creation, God's first provision to human beings is regarding food (Gen 1:29). The first prohibition is regarding not eating of the fruit of knowledge of good and evil, which later led to the first sin (Gen 2:17). After Noah comes out of the ark, God reinstates a provision and prohibition, this time allowing humans to eat meat without its lifeblood (Gen 9:3–4). Then the Israelites are instructed for Passover to eat a lamb, bread without yeast with bitter herbs, and to do it all in haste (Exod 12). In the wilderness, the Israelite's first complaint is pertaining food. Then they are fed with manna from heaven (Exod 16). Then they are given prescriptions determining which foods are considered clean to eat and which are not (Lev 11). Then Jesus' first temptation is regarding bread (Matt 4:3). Jesus then teaches his disciples to pray by saying, "Give us this day our daily bread" (Matt 6:11). He also miraculously feeds five thousand (Matt 14:13–21). And finally, the whole culinary manual culminates with the institution of the Lord's Supper.

Why does food have so much prominence in a sacred text? One would think that the Holy Book is about spiritual matters, not the mundane and physical. But the reality is that eating is a central aspect of our humanity.

Not only does our very life depend on our eating, but so much of it is spent trying to put bread on the table. Perhaps we have lost this affinity for food, given that today we can readily buy instant food and eat it in solitude. Many of us do so in our busy and lonely lives. Those of us who opt for healthier options cook our food, but ready-made ingredients and sophisticated kitchens make it easy to cook on our own. Yet, cooking was and is fundamentally a social task. Thomas O'Loughlin observes that we are the only creatures that cook our food. The cooking process involves society. In the past it was always a communal task with several gathered around the kitchen. We must keep in mind that even the ready-made ingredients available at a grocery store today were made by other people. No one individual really cooks everything from scratch. Human food therefore "presupposes society, it creates society, and it projects a vision of society."[231] Not only is cooking a social task, but traditionally eating a meal was always a shared experience fundamental to our humanity. In our modern world, where the hippest condos don't have a dining room anymore, we seem so distanced from this practice. But in all cultures of the past, people always gathered around a meal, which was seen as a sign of fellowship and hospitality. Is it any surprise then that food has such prominence in the Bible?

How then does it all culminate in the Lord's Supper? The Eucharist is the meal of all meals that looks forward to the eschatological banquet in heaven (Matt 22:1–14). It is in this meal that all of the sacrifice, the labor of our hands, fellowship, community, and hospitality come together. I already laid out how the Eucharist rebukes our individualistic consumerism. But this meal should also shed light on some of the more general economics regarding the church. All ancient societies were agrarian economies, of which even the Roman Empire was no exception. It is likely that in such economies roughly 90 percent of the population were involved in agriculture.[232] Moreover, based on the context of First Corinthians regarding hunger and drunkenness, it is likely that in the early church the Lord's Supper was an actual meal eaten at someone's private home.[233] All of this means that Communion involved the whole community bringing in food and sharing from the labor of their hands. Today it's not that big of a big deal to spend twenty bucks to share a meal when that is a minimal part of our overall budget. But in an agrarian society, to bring in a meal to share with others was not only directly the fruit of one's labor, but also a much larger share of one's income. Thus when the early church broke bread together, it was all part of them sharing their possessions with one another. In their Communion, the whole economy of its members was brought together. The Eucharist, in that sense, is literally the economy of salvation.

What would it mean for us to see the Eucharist in this way for our times? I do not want to be misunderstood. I am not arguing that the liturgical aspect of Communion as a ceremony be taken away. Nor am I suggesting that people should bring to the Communion table the microchips, toaster ovens, or whatever else they produce in their work. That would be sacrilegious. But if we have some interpretive imagination, the Eucharist does teach us that the church should have more of its hands meddling in our economic lives. We may not bring microchips to the liturgy, but we are to have at the church's disposal the fruits and skills of our labor. We are to be a true politics that reflects on the goods we have in common and how we are to distribute them rightly. Some of these goods I have mentioned in this book include but are not limited to welfare, healthcare, education, and just plain creating meaningful jobs. Hauerwas was right in saying that the Eucharist is an essential ritual of our politics. Only in the light of the Eucharist can we see the church rightly for everything that it should be. It is only when we do so that the church will not just play a peripheral role on social Sundays, but claim our hearts, minds, souls, and the entirety of our lives, as it should.

Endnotes

A DISQUIETING SUGGESTION

1. See Alan Cooperman, Gregory Smith, and Katherine Ritchey, "America's Changing Religious Landscape: Christians Decline Sharply as Share of Population; Unaffiliated and Other Faiths Continue to Grow" (Washington, DC: Pew Research Center, 2015; http://www.pewforum.org/2015/05/12/americas-changing-religious-landscape/), 3. Here, evangelicals are the only major Christian group that can claim they are not shrinking so precipitously. Yet, in proportion to the general population they are still contributing to the general decline. Moreover, evangelicals generally have more children than many other Christian groups, which greatly helps their numbers. (See Mark Chavez, *American Religion: Contemporary Trends*, 2nd ed. [Princeton, NJ: Princeton University Press, 2017], 98). This should caution evangelicals from congratulating each other. Their numbers may be more related to their birth rate than their retention rate.

2. Cooperman et al., "America's Changing Religious Landscape," 7.

3. Cooperman et al., "America's Changing Religious Landscape," 11.

4. See Karl Vaters, "If You're Voting for Trump You Can Unfriend Me (But I Hope You Won't)," *Christianity Today*, February 24, 2016 (https://www.christianitytoday.com/karl-vaters/2016/february/voting-for-trump-you-can-unfriend-me-but-i-hope-you-dont.html); and Mariam Williams, "Blocking or Keeping Friends Out of Christian 'Love,'" *National Catholic Reporter*, October 3, 2016 (https://

www.ncronline.org/blogs/intersection/blocking-or-keeping-online-friends-out-christian-love).

5. See Figure 8.1 in Chavez, *American Religion*, 102.

6. Italics added. All biblical are from the NRSV, unless otherwise indicated.

7. James Twitchell, *Shopping for God: How Christianity Went from in Your Heart to in Your Face* (New York: Simon and Schuster, 2007), 254.

8. See chapter 5 in Chavez, *American Religion*.

9. Greg L. Hawkins and Cally Parkinson, *Reveal: Where Are You?* (Barrington: Willow Creek Resources, 2007), 54.

10. Chavez, *American Religion*, 74.

11. Gerardo Marti and Gladys Ganiel, *The Deconstructed Church: Understanding Emerging Christianity* (New York: Oxford University Press, 2014), 1–5.

12. See Wes Markofski, *New Monasticism and the Transformation of American Evangelicalism* (New York: Oxford University Press, 2015).

13. Cooperman et al., "America's Changing Religious Landscape," 4.

14. Ross Douthat, "Save the Mainline," *New York Times*, April 15, 2017 (https://www.nytimes.com/2017/04/15/opinion/sunday/save-the-mainline.html).

15. Sarah Pulliam Bailey, "White Evangelicals Voted Overwhelmingly for Donald Trump," *Washington Post*, November 9, 2016 (https://www.washingtonpost.com/news/acts-of-faith/wp/2016/11/09/exit-polls-show-white-evangelicals-voted-overwhelmingly-for-donald-trump/?noredirect=on&utm_term=.e56e8271edaf).

16. Stanley Hauerwas, "Reforming Christian Social Ethics: Ten Theses," in *The Hauerwas Reader*, eds. John Berkman and Michael Cartwright (Durham: Duke University Press), 114.

17. Stanley Hauerwas, "The Servant Community: Christian Social Ethics," in Berkman and Cartwright, eds., *Hauerwas Reader*, 374.

18. Hauerwas, "Servant Community," 377.

19. Hauerwas, "Servant Community," 385.

20. Chavez, *American Religion*, 38–39.
21. Stanley Hauerwas, "Preaching as Though We Had Enemies," *First Things*, May 1995 (https://www.firstthings.com/article/1995/05/003-preaching-as-though-we-had-enemies).
22. William T. Cavanaugh, *Theopolitical Imagination: Discovering the Liturgy as a Political Act in an Age of Global Consumerism* (London: Bloomsbury Academic, 2002), 1.
23. See William T. Cavanaugh, *Being Consumed: Economics and Christian Desire* (Grand Rapids: Eerdmans, 2008).

HOW WE GOT HERE

24. Brad Gregory, *The Unintended Reformation: How a Religious Revolution Secularized Society* (Cambridge, MA: Harvard University Press, 2012), 130.
25. Gregory, *Unintended Reformation*, 150–51.
26. See Martin Luther, "To the Christian Nobility of the German Nation," in *Three Treatises* (Philadelphia, Fortress, 1988).
27. Martin Luther, "Against the Murdering and Robbing Hordes of Peasants," in *The German Reformation and the Peasant's War*, ed. Michael G. Baylor (Boston: Bedford/St. Martin's, 2012), 133.
28. Wayne P. Te Brake, *Religious War and Religious Peace in Early Modern Europe* (Cambridge: Cambridge University Press, 2017), 256.
29. Te Brake, *Religious War*, 158.
30. Cavanaugh, *Theopolitical Imagination*, 22.
31. Cavanaugh, *Theopolitical Imagination*, 25.
32. Cavanaugh, *Theopolitical Imagination*, 25.
33. See Martin Luther, *On Secular Authority*, ed. Harro Hopfl (Cambridge: Cambridge University Press: 1991).
34. Stanley Hauerwas and William H. Willimon, *Resident Aliens* (Nashville: Abingdon Press, 1989), 12.
35. Thomas Hobbes, *Leviathan* 1.13.
36. Hobbes, *Leviathan* 1.13.

37. Cavanaugh, *Theopolitical Imagination*, 10–15.
38. See Jean-Jacques Rousseau, *The Social Contract and Discourses*, trans. G. D. H. Cole (London: Everyman, 1993).
39. John Locke, *Second Treatise* 7.87.
40. See Montesquieu, *The Spirit of the Laws*.
41. Jeremy Waldron, *God, Locke, and Equality* (Cambridge: Cambridge University Press, 2002), 25.
42. U.S. Constitution, preamble.
43. U.S. Declaration of Independence.
44. Alexis de Tocqueville, *Democracy in America*, trans. Arthur Goldhammer (New York: Library of America, 2004), 3.
45. De Tocqueville, *Democracy*, 503.
46. Paul Johnson, *A History of the American People* (New York: Harper Perennial, 1999), 722–23.
47. Howard Zinn, *A People's History of the United States* (New York: HarperCollins, 2003), 125.
48. See Reinhold Niebuhr, *Moral Man and Immoral Society*, in *Reinhold Niebuhr: Major Works on Religion and Politics*, ed. Elisabeth Sifton (New York: Library of America), 135–350.
49. Stanley Hauerwas, *With the Grain of the Universe* (Grand Rapids: Brazos, 2002), 137.
50. Benjamin Carter Hett, *The Death of Democracy* (New York: Holt, 2018), 96.
51. Steven B. Webb, *Hyperinflation and Stabilization in Weimar Germany* (New York: Oxford University Press, 1989), 105.
52. Webb, *Hyperinflation*, 3.
53. Richard J. Overy, *War and Economy in the Third Reich* (New York: Oxford University Press, 1994), 182–83.
54. Robert P. Ericksen, "Assessing the Heritage: German Protestant Theologians, Nazis, and the Jewish Question," in *Betrayal: German Churches and the Holocaust*, ed. Robert P. Ericksen and Susannah Heschel (Minneapolis: Augsburg Fortress, 1999), 22.

55. Paul Althaus, in "Assessing the Heritage," 24.

56. Ericksen, "Assessing the Heritage," 27–28.

57. John Bear, "Ann Coulter Attacks Immigrants, Muslims, Prompts Walkout of CU Boulder Speech," *Denver Post*, March 22, 2018 (https://www.denverpost.com/2018/03/22/ann-coulter-cu-boulder/).

58. Richard Eskow, "Open Borders: A Gimmick, Not a Solution," BernieSanders.com, August 5, 2015 (https://berniesanders.com/open-borders-a-gimmick-not-a-solution).

59. Anna O. Law, "This Is How Trump's Deportations Differ from Obama's," *Washington Post*, May 3, 2017 (https://www.washingtonpost.com/news/monkey-cage/wp/2017/05/03/this-is-how-trumps-deportations-differ-from-obamas/?noredirect=on&utm_term=.624bd55ed123).

WHERE WE ARE

60. United Nations, *United Nations Millennium Development Goals Report*, 2015 (http://www.un.org/millenniumgoals/2015_MDG_Report/pdf/MDG%202015%20rev%20(July%201).pdf).

61. United Nations, *Millennium Development Goals*.

62. Don Peck, *Pinched: How the Great Recession Has Narrowed Our Future and What We Can Do About It* (New York: Crown, 2011), 12.

63. See Figure 5 in Thomas Picketty, Emmanuel Saez, and Gabriel Zucman, "Distributional National Accounts: Methods and Estimates for the United States," National Bureau of Economic Research Working Paper 22945, December 2016 (http://www.nber.org/papers/w22945.pdf).

64. See Cavanaugh, *Being Consumed*, 49.

65. Cavanaugh, *Being Consumed*, 47.

66. That scenario was provided by James Sandel in "Justice: The Moral Side of Murder," Harvard University, September 4, 2009 (video of lecture, https://www.youtube.com/watch?v=kBdfcR-8hEY).

67. See also Daniel J. Harrington and James F. Keenan, *Paul and Virtue Ethics* (Plymouth, RI: Rowan and Littlefield, 2010), 15.

68. See also Harrington and Keenan, *Paul and Virtue Ethics*, 110.
69. Aristotle, *Nicomachean Ethics* 2.30.
70. Kathy Gurchiek, "Millennial's Desire to Do Good Defines Workplace Culture," Society for Human Resources Managament, July 7, 2014 (https://www.shrm.org/resourcesandtools/hr-topics/behavioral-competencies/global-and-cultural-effectiveness/pages/millennial-impact.aspx).
71. Adam Smiley Poswolsky, "What Millenial Employees Really Want," *Fast Company*, June 4, 2015 (https://www.fastcompany.com/3046989/what-millennial-employees-really-want).
72. "About," Tesla.com (https://www.tesla.com/about).
73. "About," SpaceX.com (https://www.spacex.com/about).
74. Lee Hardy, *The Fabric of This World* (Grand Rapids: Eerdmans, 1990), 122.
75. Timothy Keller, *Every Good Endeavor* (New York: Dutton, 2012), 162–63.
76. Keller, *Every Good Endeavor*, 169.
77. Keller, *Every Good Endeavor*, 166.
78. John Paul II, *Laborem Exercens* 2.4, September 14, 1981 (http://w2.vatican.va/content/john-paul-ii/en/encyclicals/documents/hf_jp-ii_enc_14091981_laborem-exercens.html).
79. Augustine, *De Civitate Dei* 15.17.
80. Aristotle, *Nicomachean Ethics* 8.1–3.
81. Hauerwas and Willimon, *Resident Aliens*, 93.
82. David Hume, *A Treatise of Human Nature* 1.2 (London: Penguin, 1969), 124.
83. Hume, *Treatise of Human Nature* 1.3 (pp. 82–83).
84. Daisuke Wakabayashi and Scott Shane, "Google Will Not Renew Pentagon Contract that Upset Employees," *New York Times*, June 1, 2018 (https://www.nytimes.com/2018/06/01/technology/google-pentagon-project-maven.html).
85. Molley McCluskey, "Public Universities Get an Education in Private Industry," *Atlantic*, April 3, 2017 (https://www.theatlantic.com/

86. McCluskey, "Public Universities Get an Education."

87. Paul Root Wolpe, "A Human Head Transplant Would Be Reckless and Ghastly. It's Time to Talk about It," *Vox*, June 12, 2018 (https://www.vox.com/the-big-idea/2018/4/2/17173470/human-head-transplant-canavero-ethics-bioethics).

88. Alex Hern, "Elon Musk Says He Invested in DeepMind over 'Terminator' Fears," *Guardian*, June 18, 2014 (https://www.theguardian.com/technology/2014/jun/18/elon-musk-deepmind-ai-tesla-motors); and Samuel Gibbs, "Elon Musk: Artificial Intelligence Is Our Biggest Existential Threat," *Guardian*, October 27, 2014 (https://www.theguardian.com/technology/2014/oct/27/elon-musk-artificial-intelligence-ai-biggest-existential-threat).

89. Nick Statt, "Elon Musk Launches Neuralink, a Venture to Merge the Human Brain with AI," *Verge*, March 27, 2017 (https://www.theverge.com/2017/3/27/15077864/elon-musk-neuralink-brain-computer-interface-ai-cyborgs).

WHERE WE CAME FROM

90. See Rob Barret, *Disloyalty and Destruction* (Library of Hebrew Bible/Old Testament Studies; New York: T. & T. Clark, 2009), 511.

91. David Briggs, "The Financial Crisis Facing U.S. Churches," *Huffington Post*, November 6, 2016 (https://www.huffingtonpost.com/david-briggs/the-financial-crisis-faci_b_8481434.html).

92. Barrett, *Disloyalty*, 61.

93. The book of Esther shows some of the compromises some Israelites may have made with the dominant culture.

94. Anathea Portier-Young, *Apocalypse Against Empire* (Grand Rapids: Eerdmans, 2011), 223.

95. William T. Cavanaugh, *Migrations of the Holy* (Grand Rapids: Eerdmans, 2011), 105.

96. See Stanley Hauerwas, "Peacemaking: The Virtue of the Church," in Berkman and Cartwright, eds., *Hauerwas Reader*, 318.

97. N. T. Wright, *Simply Christian* (New York: HaperOne, 2006), 161.
98. Wright, *Simply Christian*, 160.
99. N. T. Wright, *Surprised by Hope* (New York: HarperOne, 2008), 231.
100. See also John Howard Yoder, *The Politics of Jesus*, 2nd ed. (Grand Rapids: Eerdmans, 1993), 25.
101. Yoder, *Politics of Jesus*, 29.
102. Yoder, *Politics of Jesus*, 34.
103. Yoder, *Politics of Jesus*, 34.
104. Yoder, *Politics of Jesus*, 67–68.
105. Yoder, *Politics of Jesus*, 70–71.
106. Yoder, *Politics of Jesus*, 112–26.
107. Kavin Rowe, *World Upside Down* (New York: Oxford University Press, 2009), 5.
108. Rowe, *World Upside Down*, 73–74.
109. Rowe, *World Upside Down*, 61.
110. Benedict, *The Rule of Saint Benedict* 48, trans. Justin McCann (Westminster: Christian Classics, 1978), 53.
111. F. R. Cowell, *Everyday Life in Ancient Rome* (London: B. T. Badsford, 1966), 97.
112. Cicero, *De Officiis* 1.150.
113. Randall Collins, *Weberian Sociological Theory* (New York: Cambridge University Press, 1986), 57.
114. Collins, *Weberian Sociological Theory*, 55.
115. Jean Gimpel, *The Medieval Machine* (New York: Rinehart and Winston, 1976) 3–5.
116. Gimpel, *Medieval Machine*, 67–68.
117. Gimpel, *Medieval Machine*, 68.
118. Collins, *Weberian Sociological Theory*, 54.
119. Collins, *Weberian Sociological Theory*, 55.
120. Gimpel, *Medieval Machine*, 52.

121. Diane Wood, *Medieval Economic Thought* (Cambridge: Cambridge University Press, 2002), 26.

122. Wood, *Medieval Economic Thought*, 132-58.

123. Ralph W. Mathisen, "Bishops, Barbarians, and the 'Dark Ages': The Fate of Late Roman Educational Institutions in Late Antique Gaul," in *Medieval Education*, ed. Ronald B. Begley and Joseph W. Koterski (New York: Fordham University Press, 2005), 3.

124. Mathisen, "Bishops, Barbarians, and the "Dark Ages," 10.

125. Mathisen, "Bishops, Barbarians, and the "Dark Ages," 12.

126. Benedict, *Rules* 48.

127. W. G. Hanson, *The Early Monastic Schools of Ireland* (New York: Lenox Hill, 1972), 3–4.

128. Tania D. Ivanova-Sullivan, "Interpreting Medieval Literacy: Learning and Education in *Slavia Orthodoxa* (Bulgaria) and Byzantium in the Ninth to Twelfth Centuries," in Begley and Koterski, eds. *Medieval Education*, 51.

129. Benedict. M. Ashley, *The Dominicans* (Collegeville, MN: Liturgical, 1990), 12.

130. Ashley, *Dominicans*, 23–24.

131. Ashley, *Dominicans*, 35.

132. Walter Ruegg, ed., *Universities in the Middle Ages*, vol. 1 of *A History of the University in Europe* (Cambridge: Cambridge University Press, 1992), 15.

133. Ruegg, *Universities in the Middle Ages*, 16.

134. Ruegg, *Universities in the Middle Ages*, 32.

135. Ruegg, *Universities in the Middle Ages*, 32–33.

136. James Hannam, *The Genesis of Science* (Washington, DC: Regnery, 2011), 56–57.

137. Hannam, *Genesis of Science*, 93.

138. Hannam, *Genesis of Science*, 159.

139. Hannam, *Genesis of Science*, 181.

140. Hannam, *Genesis of Science*, 179–80.

141. Hannam, *Genesis of Science*, 182–83.
142. Hannam, *Genesis of Science*, 218.
143. Hannam, *Genesis of Science*, 277.
144. Hannam, *Genesis of Science*, 293.
145. Hannam, *Genesis of Science*, 327.
146. Hannam, *Genesis of Science*, 326.
147. Hannam, *Genesis of Science*, 331–32.
148. Eusebius, *Ecclesiastical History* 2.7.7–10.
149. Eusebius, *Ecclesiastical History* 2.7.7–10.
150. Guenter B. Risse, *Mending Bodies, Saving Souls* (New York: Oxford University Press, 1999), 80.
151. Risse, *Mending Bodies*, 80.
152. Risse, *Mending Bodies*, 81.
153. Risse, *Mending Bodies*, 81.
154. Risse, *Mending Bodies*, 94.
155. Risse, *Mending Bodies*, 95.
156. Risse, *Mending Bodies*, 77.
157. Hannam, *Genesis of Science*, 255–56.
158. Risse, *Mending Bodies*, 85.
159. Barbra Mann Wall, *Unlikely Entrepreneurs: Catholic Sisters and the Hospital Marketplace, 1865–1925* (Columbus: Ohio State University Press, 2005), 195.
160. Stanley Hauerwas, "Romans 13," video, produced by Third Way, (https://www.youtube.com/results?search_query=Hauerwas+Romans+13).
161. Yoder, *Politics of Jesus*, 44–45.
162. As quoted by Richard Hays in *Echoes of Scripture in the Gospels* (Waco, TX: Baylor University Press, 2016), 27.
163. Richard B. Hays, *Reading Backwards* (Waco, TX: Baylor University Press, 2014), 7.
164. Hays, *Echoes of Scripture in the Gospels*, 28.

WHERE TO GO FROM HERE

165. Anya Kamenetz, "How Socioeconomic Diversity Helps All Students." *KQED News*, March 16, 2017 (https://www.kqed.org/mindshift/47765/how-socioeconomic-diversity-in-schools-helps-all-students).

166. Stanley Hauerwas, *The Peaceable Kingdom* (London: SCM, 2003), 108.

167. Stanley Hauerwas, "Home for Good Stanley Hauerwas," video, produced by Home for Good, 5.15. (https://www.youtube.com/watch?v=xIhoVIs-6ns).

168. Muhammad Yunus, *A World of Three Zeros* (New York: Public Affairs, 2017), 23.

169. Yunus, *A World of Three Zeros*, 27.

170. Yunus, *A World of Three Zeros*, 81–82.

171. Yunus, *A World of Three Zeros*, 37–38.

172. Yunus, *A World of Three Zeros*, 85–87.

173. Yunus, *A World of Three Zeros*, 10–12.

174. Yunus, *A World of Three Zeros*, 8.

175. Yunus, *A World of Three Zeros*, 69–71.

176. Yunus, *A World of Three Zeros*, 150–51.

177. David Gelles, James B. Stewart, Jessica Silver-Greenbeg, and Kate Kelly, "Elon Musk Details 'Excruciating' Personal Toll of Tesla Turmoil," *New York Times*, August 16, 2018 (https://www.nytimes.com/2018/08/16/business/elon-musk-interview-tesla.html).

178. Emily Stewart, "Elon Musk's Week of Pot Smoking and Wild Emails, Explained," *Vox*, September 8, 2018 (https://www.vox.com/business-and-finance/2018/9/8/17834910/elon-musk-joe-rogan-podcast-tesla-stock).

179. Sam Levin, "Elon Musk Calls British Diver in Thai Cave Rescue 'Pedo' in Baseless Attack," *Guardian*, July 16, 2018 (https://www.theguardian.com/technology/2018/jul/15/elon-musk-british-diver-thai-cave-rescue-pedo-twitter).

180. Jackie Watters, "Elon Musk Mocks SEC amid Settlement Deal," *CNN*, October 4, 2018 (https://www.cnn.com/2018/10/04/business/elon-musk-sec-settlement/index.html).

181. Michael Grothaus, "Dozens of Tesla Employees Have Jumped Ship to Apple," *Fast Company*, August, 24, 2018 (https://www.fastcompany.com/90226090/dozens-of-tesla-employees-have-jumped-ship-to-apple).

182. Michael Sainato, "Tesla Workers Speak Out: 'Anything Pro-Union Is Shut Down Really Fast,'" *Guardian*, September 10, 2018 (https://www.theguardian.com/technology/2018/sep/10/tesla-workers-union-elon-musk).

183. Ashlee Vance, *Elon Musk and the Quest for a Fantastic Future* (New York: HaperCollins, 2017), 22–23.

184. Vance, *Elon Musk*, 29–30.

185. Vance, *Elon Musk*, 32.

186. Vance, *Elon Musk*, 33.

187. Vance, *Elon Musk*, 35.

188. Vance, *Elon Musk*, 19–21.

189. Vance, *Elon Musk*, 38–39.

190. Vance, *Elon Musk*, 43–62.

191. Vance, *Elon Musk*, 64–73.

192. Nadia Drake, "Elon Musk: In Seven Years, SpaceX Could Land Humans on Mars," *National Geographic*, September 29, 2017 (https://news.nationalgeographic.com/2017/09/elon-musk-spacex-mars-moon-bfr-rockets-space-science/).

193. Vance, *Elon Musk*, 40.

194. Vance, *Elon Musk*, 74–84.

195. Vance, *Elon Musk*, 91.

196. Vance, *Elon Musk*, 110–33.

197. Vance, *Elon Musk*, 106–9.

198. Vance, *Elon Musk*, 136.

199. Vance, *Elon Musk*, 159.

200. Vance, *Elon Musk*, 160.

201. Vance, *Elon Musk*, 154.

202. Vance, *Elon Musk*, 164.

203. Vance, *Elon Musk*, 164; and Owen Thomas, "Tesla's Elon Musk: 'I Ran out of Cash,'" *VentureBeat*, May 27, 2010 (https://venturebeat.com/2010/05/27/elon-musk-personal-finances/)

204. Loren Grush, "A Successful SpaceX Falcon Heavy Launch Gives NASA New Options," *Verge*, February 2, 2018 (https://www.theverge.com/2018/2/2/16954582/spacex-falcon-heavy-rocket-launch-impact-nasa-deep-space-travel); and Mike Wall, "NASA's Huge New Rocket May Cost $500 Million per Launch," *Space*, September 12, 2012 (https://www.space.com/17556-giant-nasa-rocket-space-launch-cost.html).

205. Darrell Etherington, "SpaceX Plans to Use Spaceships for Earth Passenger Transit," *TechCrunch*, October 2017 (https://techcrunch.com/2017/09/28/spacex-plans-to-use-spaceships-for-earth-passenger-transit/).

206. Kevin Kelleher, "How Cheap Internet Access Could Be SpaceX's Secret Weapon," *Time*, January 18, 2017 (http://time.com/4638470/spacex-internet-elon-musk/).

207. Mike Snider, "A Victory for Elon Musk: Tesla Outsells Mercedes-Benz in US for First Time Ever," *USA Today*, October 11, 2018 (https://www.usatoday.com/story/money/nation-now/2018/10/11/tesla-outsells-mercedes-benz-elon-musk/1598474002/).

208. US Environmental Protection Agency, "Fast Facts on Transportation Greenhouse Gas Emissions" (https://www.epa.gov/greenvehicles/fast-facts-transportation-greenhouse-gas-emissions).

209. Diane Rado, "New Education Funding Law Could Be Lifeline to Private Schools," *Chicago Tribune*, September 2, 2017 (http://www.chicagotribune.com/news/ct-private-school-tax-credits-met-20170901-story.html).

210. Isabella O'Malley, "Making Plastic Out of the Air Pollution We Breathe," *Weather Network*, May 25, 2018 (https://www.theweathernetwork.com/us/news/articles/

making-plastic-out-of-the-air-pollution-we-breathe-carbon-climate-change-global-warming-ocean-ethylene/102321).

211. Elizabeth Weise, "It Took 5 Years, Now the Ocean Cleanup System Is Heading to the Great Pacific Garbage Patch," *USA Today*, September 9, 2018 (https://www.usatoday.com/story/tech/science/2018/09/09/ocean-cleanup-system-heading-great-pacific-garbage-patch/1243172002/).

212. T. R. Reid, "How We Spend $3,400,000,000,000," *Atlantic*, June 15, 2017 (https://www.theatlantic.com/health/archive/2017/06/how-we-spend-3400000000000/530355/).

213. See Melissa D. Aldridge and Amy S. Kelley, "The Myth Regarding the High Cost of End-of-Life Care," *American Journal of Public Health* 105/12 (December 2015) 2411–15; and Eric B. French et al., "End-Of-Life Medical Spending in Last Twelve Months Oof Life Is Lower than Previously Reported," *Health Affairs* 36/7 (July 2017) (https://www.healthaffairs.org/doi/full/10.1377/hlthaff.2017.0174).

214. Stanley Hauerwas, *Naming the Silences* (New York: T. & T. Clark, 2004), 101.

215. Allen Verhey, *The Christian Art of Dying* (Grand Rapids: Eerdmans, 2011), 17.

216. Michael B. Rothberg et al., "The Cost of Defensive Medicine on Three Hospital Medicine Services," *JAMA Internal Medicine* 174/11 (November 1, 2014) 1867–68.

217. Lisa Schenker, "Frustrated with Health Insurance Costs, Some Turn to Religious Plans: 'For Us It's Been a Godsend,'" *Chicago Tribune*, October 14, 2018 (http://www.chicagotribune.com/business/ct-biz-religious-health-care-cost-sharing-1014-story.html).

218. See Elisabeth Rosenthal, "In Need of a New Hip, but Priced Out of the US," *New York Times*, August 3, 2013 (https://www.nytimes.com/2013/08/04/health/for-medical-tourists-simple-math.html). A hip replacement in the U.S. would have cost around $100,000, whereas the same procedure in Belgium (not the cheapest of countries) costs $13,000.

219. Mike Holmes, "What Would Happen If the Church Tithed?," *Relevant Magazine*, March 8, 2016 (https://relevantmagazine.com/love-and-money/what-would-happen-if-church-tithed).

220. Ronald J. Sider, *Rich Christians in an Age of Hunger* (Nashville: T. Nelson, 2005), 187–90.

221. Rebecca Y. Kim, *The Spirit Moves West* (New York: Oxford University Press, 2015), 33.

222. Stanley Hauerwas, "Why Community Is Dangerous, an Interview," interview by Peter Mommsen, *Plough Quarterly*, March 4, 2016 (https://www.plough.com/en/topics/community/church-community/why-community-is-dangerous).

EPILOGUE

223. Hauerwas, *Peaceable Kingdom*, 108.

224. Hauerwas, *Peaceable Kingdom*, 108.

225. Marti and Ganiel, *Deconstructed Church*, 126–67.

226. Marti and Ganiel, *Deconstructed Church*, 125.

227. Richard B. Hays, *First Corinthians* (Interpretation; Louisville: John Knox, 1997), 137.

228. Hays, *First Corinthians*, 142.

229. Kelley Holland, "Fighting with Your Spouse? It's Probably about This," *CNBC*, February 4, 2015 (https://www.cnbc.com/2015/02/04/money-is-the-leading-cause-of-stress-in-relationships.html).

230. Lauren F. Winner, *Wearing God* (New York: HarperOne, 2015), 92.

231. Thomas O'Laughlin, *The Eucharist: Origins and Contemporary Understandings* (Chennai: Bloomsbury, 2015), 62.

232. Neville Morley, *Metropolis and Hinterland* (Cambridge: Cambridge University Press, 1996), 13.

233. Hays, *First Corinthians*, 193.